Author's father and friends at deer camp

Visit

www.heroesinplaid.com

for more information on the author, special offers, and to receive updates on new titles by D.S. Taylor

Author's father, grandfather, and family friend at deer camp

In many cases, being a hero is not because of the way a person died, but because of the way they lived their life, with character, integrity, honor, and love.

Author's father Gordon and Uncle Jack

Proverbs 28:6 - Better is the one of little means who is walking in his integrity, than anyone crooked in his ways, although he is rich.

Dedication

This book is dedicated to the heroes who came along early in my life:

My father who instilled a sense of wonder and love for the outdoors before he went to be with his maker when he was only thirty-six-years young.
My mother who raised us and allowed us to pursue that love.
My grandparents, aunts, and uncles who kept us in the woods and on the water hunting and fishing until we were old enough to go on our own.
My loving wife who never said "no" when I wanted to go off on one of these trips and who always figured out how I could afford it when I probably should have stayed home.
My children who gave up so much of their time with me so I could go to the woods.
My three brothers whose hunting and fishing knowledge and genuine concern for my success has made every one of my trips successful.
My buddy Steve and the other guys I share camps with who invite me back year after year.
All those farmers who let us take rod and gun upon their land and pursue our passions.
The policemen, firemen, and paramedics who rush into danger when we are rushing out and allow us to sleep in peace at night.
The unselfish young men and women who wear the military camo and risk their lives or die to allow me to live in a free country and hold the rights I so often take for granted.
The missionaries who risk their lives to spread the gospel.
To all those parents, relatives, friends, and mentors who get their own kids or someone else's into the woods and on the waters in search of a good time afield.
And to Nicole for dotting my I's crossing my T's and making my jargon legible.

I am sure I have forgotten countless others - thank you so much.

CONTENTS

CONTENTS

Forward

If you were to look up the word *hero* in the dictionary, you would find that Webster used these words to describe what a hero is: "To watch over and protect. Any person admired for courage, nobility, or exploits especially in war. Any person admired for qualities or achievements and regarded as an ideal or model. The central figure in any important event or period honored for outstanding qualities."

Webster goes on in his description of a hero, but he leaves out a few things I think are important in defining a hero. Through my involvement with a leadership development company called TEAM, I have learned a lot more about heroes and would have to include this: I believe a hero could be a guide in our lives who keeps us on the right path. A person who illustrates our highest values; someone we look up to. Not someone who dazzles us, but someone who enlarges us and makes us better for having known them. Someone who themselves has a largeness of character and moral ethics, a bigness of spirit. They are unselfish; strong yet gentle; act out of a sense of duty, not for glory; and have a humble spirit and are free of arrogance. We look up to our heroes and in doing so, we are drawn up.

Everyone I have written about on these pages embodies these qualities. They are heroes in my life and for that, I am forever grateful.

The first heroes in my life, and the ones this book is titled after, were those who stepped up to help my brothers and me learn to enjoy the great outdoors. They came from multiple walks of life yet all had something in common. Each fall around November 15 they would don their red and black plaid hunting suits. They were made of wool and sewn by Woolrich. These heroes would get outdoors and chase the elusive whitetail buck, and they always made sure my brothers and I were included.

Yes, my heroes wore Woolrich and dressed in red plaid.

Gone By The Wayside

The farther I get away from the wilderness, as the trees begin to disappear, I find myself shorter on words. As the woods and wild creatures become scarce so does my conversation as well as my patience. I know the woods and I know the wild things, but I have very little knowledge of the city and for that matter, very little interest. I feel at home in the woods and I never feel lonely, but put me in a city full of people and I feel restless and very much alone. I feel alienated and vulnerable and don't care to blend in and become a part of that way of life. I would much rather sit in a tree and watch the creatures go about their day than be trapped in some concrete jungle surrounded by un-friendly faces. A fresh ground-frost on an October morning as the sun begins to peek over the horizon, shared only with a noisy jay or busy fox squirrel, is much more appealing than a hotel or cruise liner filled with strangers who care only about themselves. Or a fancy restaurant full of scavengers who have no idea that the pheasant or duck they ordered came from a pen instead of roaming free. I'm sorry if I sound bitter here, but wildlife and the lands they inhabit are dear to me and I hate to see them thrust to the wayside because of encroaching so-called progress. I work each year to create an environment friendly to the wildlife and don't have a kind word for those developers who would turn a pleasant meadow or brushy woodlot into a subdivision or shopping mall where wildlife is pushed out and people push their way in. Call me a hick, a redneck, country bumpkin, farm boy or whatever; just don't call me civilized if destroying habitat to build a city is what civilization is all about. I am a steward of the land. A duty I gladly except, as the land has been good to me and all that I have put into it has been re-turned ten-fold. The time and money put forth is more than re-paid by a morning in the woods. The feeling of freedom and the connection with my ancestors who hunted before me are enough in itself. A fat buck for the freezer is a bonus and will never go to waste.

I grew up in the country in southern Michigan and spent many a day stalking squirrels and flushing pheasants as a young child. Now, as I drive the backroads of this state, I get a sickening feeling in my stomach, a heavy feeling in my heart, and a longing for a simpler day when everything was wild. New construction is everywhere. More and more farmers have to sell off farmland and woodlots because the prices they get for their crops are not enough to pay off ever-increasing debt. Their land is being bought up by developers who care more about their personal bank accounts than a way of life that was our heritage. Every acre that is turned into a shopping mall or a subdivision is one less acre where wildlife can roam freely. It's one less acre open to hunting, and one less acre of crops that could feed starving people. It's lost forever to the advancement of civilization that pushes itself in and wildlife out. This has been happening since the early 1900's and thank God back then someone had the foresight to do something about it. In 1937, they passed the Pittman-Robertson Bill. This bill earmarked monies taken in from excise taxes on guns and ammunitions to a wildlife restoration act. Over the years, this money has helped buy hundreds of thousands of acres of state lands open to everyone and paid for by hunters. This money does not help the small-time farmers however, and they are forced to sell their land to make ends meet. I remember as a young lad walking miles of fencerows teaming with rabbits, pheasants, and quail and sneaking along miles of winding streambeds for waterfowl. Doing chores like baling hay and straw, cutting weeds and corn out of bean fields, or picking rocks—all for hunting rights instead of cash. We were paying back grateful farmers with a rabbit or plump pheasant for their dinner table and having them thank us for the meat, when in fact it was us boys who were grateful for the privilege to walk upon their land with guns in hand to hunt their precious game. Most of that land now holds houses and businesses instead of wildlife. And most of the proud farmers who labored over their land and left it wildlife friendly now look out their windows at rows of houses which are full of strangers who know little or care little about their neighbors, both human and wildlife. I have seen the tears in a farmer's eyes at auctions where their land is being sold, realizing their children will not have that land to carry on a family tradition of turning fertile ground into something as beautiful as a field of wheat waving in a gentle breeze or rows of corn stalks, all reaching skyward asking for rain. And I have seen that same lost look in their eyes as they watch woodlots where they used to squirrel hunt with their grandfathers being burned and bulldozed. The woodlots they hoped to someday do the same with their grandkids because of the lasting impression it made on their own lives. The very places that had become such a huge part of themselves, that they had hoped to pass on to the next generations, were now sold to someone who will more than likely rape it of its beauty and forever change its purpose of sustaining a wilder side of nature. I am sure our Forefathers and even the Lord himself are frowning as they look down on this so-called progress.

I can only imagine the beauty of this land two hundred years ago as it stood tall and majestic, its virgin timber reaching high into the clear blue skies and reflecting in crystal clear waters that flowed across its country side. An abundance of wildlife that the first trappers found and the treasures of fish and unspoiled nature are known only to the natives of this land and to God himself.

I go to bed at night wondering if our Forefathers could have foreseen what would have become of their wild world. Would they have pulled that first stump and cleared that first field to build that first city?

Perhaps it is time we all sit back and reflect on what we have surrendered to our greed. Anyone long familiar with the countryside of thirty or so years ago is forced to admit that oh so very much has been lost along the wayside. The land itself is still there, but its capacity to again become habitat fit for wildlife has come close to the point of no return where resuscitation and resurrection are no longer possible.

I am a hunter and fisherman and I am grateful I live in a country where I have these privileges and can chase the wild things. Yet

I am ashamed that I am part of a culture that is destroying so much habitat and doing so very little about it. I believe I was put on this earth to help take care of its creatures and their habitat and I will do what I can to make my property more friendly to the wildlife which are themselves helpless to bail themselves out of such a dire situation.

I have my fears that the day is not far off when the sounds of a Tom Turkey's gobble, a rooster pheasant's cackle, or the yips and howls of a coyote pack, are only echoes in our memory banks and no longer heard outside our window. And the calmness and serenity that overcomes us as we gaze upon fields of wildflowers and clover dotted with grazing whitetail deer will no longer be felt unless we pack up in our cars and drive the miles to some park that has been spared the wrath of dozers and excavators. So many fence rows that the farmers of yesteryear left fat and tangled with brush, and so many grass and weed fields choked with crab apples and wild raspberries have been replaced with tight trimmed yards and concrete where not even a ground squirrel could find refuge. The clumsy beauty of a newborn fawn as it staggers to its feet, the gracefulness of a red-tailed hawk as it soars overhead, and the rainbow of colors that adorns a ringneck pheasant are all forever gone because of a selfish human race. There are a multitude of forests cut down and turned into lumber to build more unwanted houses that will choke the life out of our countryside. Where do we expect all these wild creatures to go? We give them very few options other than into the roadways where they are obliterated. And then when they do, we have insurance companies telling our DNR that we have an over abundance and we need to remove more of them because of overpopulation. It is not overpopulation you ignorant imbeciles! Do the math. Or better yet, open your eyes; it's an absence of habitat, a lack of cover, a place to live.

As a nation, we need to wake up, take a look around, and quit hiding behind our ignorance. At an alarming rate we are losing our countryside, the habitat that sustains our wildlife, and the farmland that is needed to feed a growing population.

My father passed away at the young age of thirty-six when the Lord chose to take him because cancers had ravaged his body. He left behind four strapping young boys, but had instilled in us a love for the hunt and a love of fishing that would stay with us for the rest of our days. My grandparents, uncles, aunts, and a few close friends would keep us in the woods and on the water, and further enhance that love. But if it were not for those gracious farmers who let us walk their creek banks and invade their fields and forests, we may have taken a different path in life and turned out much less than we are today. Four growing boys without a father to keep them in line had a lot of frustrations and problems to work out and most of this was done in the woods rather than on the street. Where crime or drugs and alcohol could have easily lured us into the depths of its icy waters, we chose instead to dive head first into the out-of-doors and partake in its bounty of fish and wildlife, and only because of local farmers who were kind and generous enough to allow us that opportunity. For this I am forever grateful, and I know my brothers feel the same way because to this day they still have that relationship with those same farmers or their children.

Others have told me to put my thoughts, poems, and stories into book form because someone out there might get something out of reading them. I know my stories pale in comparison to the thousands of outdoor writers who make a living doing what comes more naturally to them. I still thought that if there was a chance there were readers who could identify with my writings, then maybe I could sell a few copies and put whatever earnings I made back into the land to make it more wildlife friendly.

I have often thought of a land-share concept where a person with enough money could help bail a farmer out of debt so they could afford to keep farming their property as long as they and their children were alive and wanted to do so. The farmer would figure out what he thought was a fair price for his land minus the few acres that his house stood on. He would turn over ownership, then draw an advance on this money to pay off his debt and would get the rest when he or his kin no longer wished to farm. This would enable the farmer and his family to live a life unburdened by the stresses of debt and allow them to do what they love and have built a life around. In return, the farmer would fatten up his fence-rows and leave a small amount of grain in the fields at the end of harvest. He would also allow hunting to a reasonable amount of responsible hunters during the year. If an idea like this could be adopted by some sportsman's clubs, just think of the habitat we could save for future generations of sportsmen like ourselves. And think of the children we could help steer down a path that leads to the great outdoors and not to the pitfalls of what the city streets have in store. Any profit I make off this book will be dedicated to such a cause starting here at home and then as far as the finances will take me.

I attended a farm auction awhile back and was saddened as I watched the farmer (who was being forced to sell all he owned to pay off debt) walk about his implements and stare out across his fields. Knowing that tomorrow would bring uncertainties, and that he would no longer make a meager living from the soil, brought tears to his eyes. He wept openly and I could only begin to understand his pain and heartache. I wished there was a way I could have made a difference in his life, but I was strapped financially myself. That day I made a vow to myself that somehow, someway, I would strive to make a difference so that the small-time farmer does not completely slip into oblivion.

An aging gentleman stood beside me as I witnessed that farmer break down and I will never forget the words he so eloquently spoke: "When will they wake up and realize that cattle don't feed on concrete, corn don't grow on rooftops, and critters need room to roam?" I couldn't have said it better myself.

God bless the small time farmers and God bless you for buying this book. Your money will be well spent in an effort to bring back a little bit of yesterday in hopes of insuring a better tomorrow for our land and its bounty of wildlife that depends on us for its survival.

His Land, It Was His Life

Thirty years had come and gone
Since I left our hometown
Work and life engulfed my time
And I hadn't been around

But I heard a farmer friend was ill
And I longed to see his face
And thank him for the years he let
Me traipse about his place

Four hundred acres that he owned
Of woods and field and stream
Fence-rows and a farm pond
Rounded out a young boy's dream

Summer days and cane poles
Cut off jeans and man's best friend
Then twenty-twos and bushy tails
Would close out summer's end

Autumn promised ringnecks
And puddle jumping ducks
Then frosty morning's camo clad
Chasing elusive bucks

A couple pheasants skinned and dressed
Was payment offered up
And he graciously accepted
Though I felt it not near enough

He'd spent his lifetime on this land
He'd been here since his birth
He eked a meager living
Tilling up the earth

His son was killed in Vietnam
That heartache took his wife
All he had was farming
This land became his life

But farming wasn't paying off
Rising debt just wouldn't stop
The government had let him down
No money for his crops

And now the bank foreclosed on him
The auction was today
Everything would have to go
Even he could not stay

As I pulled down that country road
It was lined with cars and trucks
As penny-pinching heartless fools
All rummaged through his stuff

The bids called out were sickening
Selling prices a disgrace
I thought this must be killing him
So I searched for his face

I finally found him all alone
Behind his weathered shed
Leaning against a feeding trough
Where his livestock always fed

I offered him a handshake
And he forced a gentle smile
He said it's been a coon's age
I haven't seen you in awhile

So as the sale went on we talked
About how things had led to this
He said farming is a hard life
It's either hit or miss

He said I had some good years
Good seed, good sun, good rain
But when everyone has record crops
It's hard to sell your grain

And then there were the dry years
When everything went bad
Crops died off, equipment broke
The bills took all I had

So I sold a couple acres
To pay off rising debt
Now people live where corn once grew
Strangers I've never met

I used to know my neighbors
And those across the mile
And everyone who passed this house
They used to wave and smile

It isn't like that any more
Nobody seems to care
This town seems cold and distant
No neighborliness out there

My friend down at the bank has died
Now lawyers run the show
Developers all want my land
And they're forcing me to go

They're selling all I have he said
Nobody wants me here
This man I knew, so strong, so proud
Was now forcing back his tears

This auction on his land today
To him was living hell
I saw a bit of life leave him
Each time that gavel fell

They auctioned off his tractor
His truck, his disk, his plow
The furnishings inside his house
They even sold his cows

Each time that auctioneer yelled sold
Was a dagger to his heart
Now all was gone, the land was next
And with that he couldn't part

He took my hand and kissed my cheek
And in a frail voice said It's done
So long my friend for I must go
To join my wife and son

At that he drifted off to sleep
Never again to wake
The loss of his beloved land
Was more than he could take

He lost his son in Vietnam
That heartache took his wife
All he had left was farming
His land, it was his life

A Gentle Squeeze

The sun had been above the horizon for an hour or so when we finally made it into the northern Michigan hardwoods. That may seem late for an avid squirrel hunter but we thought it was pretty good timing for a father with three boys in tow. We found a nice tree that we could all sit around and instructions were given out to sit still, don't talk, and keep your eyes open for bushy tails. I remember sitting there trying so hard to be quiet and still because I was so excited to be in the woods with my dad on a hunt. An hour or so into the hunt, I was taking in the colors of autumn and I was drifting off to sleep when my father squeezed my knee and whispered "don't move a muscle." I opened my eyes expecting to see a fox squirrel coming down a tree, but instead laid my eyes on a large bobcat sneaking by just a few short yards away. To a five-year-old this cat looked as big as a lion; I never will forget the thrill of seeing that majestic animal. As I recall that hunt from my memory bank and relive it over in my mind, it seems like only yesterday. That hunt was over forty years ago and it would be the last hunt I ever shared with my father. Cancer had invaded his body, leaving him bedridden and then taken his life at the young age of thirty-six. He did manage one more hunt by himself that fall and he took a fine eight-point buck; but that's another story.

My father, like his father, was a lover of the outdoors. He loved to fish and hunt and had a zest for life in general. I believe my father knew his time was short when he took all three of us into the woods that day. Why else would you drag three noisy boys along on a hunt where the order of the day was silence and very little movement? I believe he had intentions to instill in us the passion he had for the out-of-doors. It worked like a charm; for the time in the woods that day ignited a spark that would fuel a fire that burns to this day. My brothers and I spend the first nine months of the year preparing for the hunt, and then the last three months living it, getting into the woods at every opportunity. We love to chase the whitetail deer and it has become, as my wife would say, an obsession in our lives.

My passion is bow hunting. I love to sit in a tree and watch the wild world go by, unaware of my presence. I take in a deep breath of October and pull it into my lungs. I hold it as long as I can and let it seep into the empty places of my soul, not wanting to let go of autumn. As I sit and become part of my surroundings, I feel closer to my father. When a deer is near, I feel my father's gentle squeeze upon my knee and I hear his whisper on the wind saying "Sit still and don't move a muscle." Countless times I've heard that whisper, for it is a part of the autumn woods and lingers somewhere on those gentle breezes that find their way to my anxious ears every time a deer approaches. And just as many times I've felt that gentle squeeze that sends a jolt of adrenalin surging through my body, awakening the predator that dwells inside these tired and battered bones. It brings to life all the senses that epitomize a hunter's soul. It is in this moment I feel the most alive, when I feel the closest to the ones I've lost. This is the moment where it all makes sense, a part of why I am here and how I came to be.

This is the moment we wait for all year. The weight of an uncaring world is lifted for a brief second and it takes your breath away. Your heart beats faster and you swear the deer will hear. You swallow hard and just when you think you are gaining control, your knees begin to shake. This is what brings me into the woods, this feeling of being a part of something so much greater, so much grander than the everyday life that drags us down and rubs our faces in it. My father wanted us to experience this and that is why he was willing to drag three young boys off to the woods. I think a limit of squirrels was probably the last thing on his mind that morning. And then, when he brought home that final buck atop his car and had us help him hang it up, it was another chance to instill in us a sense of wonder. He shared with us his hunt that morning and I remember asking him to repeat it several more times. It was a wild adventure to a six-year-old and I dreamt of the day I could carry a gun to the woods.

My grandfather and my uncles picked up where my father left off and fanned and fueled that spark he ignited in us. By the time we were twelve and able to carry a gun and buy a license, that spirit burned out of control like a prairie fire driven by a mighty wind. Every day during hunting season we would rush home from school and head to the woods. September 15 was a holiday to us and if our grades were up, we could take opening day of squirrel season off. The same went for the October 20 start to pheasant season and November 15 deer season opener. Those were days we never missed spending in the woods. And until now, some forty odd years later, I have only missed one opening day of deer season which was when I was in Air Force boot camp. My drill instructor couldn't get it through his thick skull why I should be allowed to take a short leave to go hunting.

What was a way of life for my grandfather and father, and many times a means of survival, is only a hobby to us. I use the word hobby only for a lack of better words. Unlike our father and grandfather, who many times had no other option but to head to the woods to feed their families, we could always go to the market and get meat. Regardless, this is a hobby we are very passionate about. One we will fight for and defend until we draw our last breath. One we will work to keep for our children and grandchildren. If you try to take this right away, you are walking on the fighting side of all of us, for we are proud of our heritage. We were blessed to have hunters in our family to teach us the ropes, and blessed to have grandmothers and a mother who would cook everything we brought home.

I often think I was born a century too late and wish we could return to a simpler, slower paced way of life where we lived off the land and got our meat sneaking through the forest rather than standing in line at some checkout counter. As for me, and I believe I speak for my brothers, we will continue to hunt until we can no longer make it to the woods. I look forward to every autumn and every hunt. And as always, that gentle squeeze on my knee and welcome breeze that whispers, "Sit still and don't move a muscle."

That first hunt was a life changing event for me and can be the same for most children. So take a kid to the woods and help them learn to enjoy the wild side. Be a mentor and share the experience with a child. They won't forget it.

Forever Grateful

Forward
to
A Moment in Her Memory

The following poem was inspired by my grandmother's bout with Alzheimer's and the effect it had on my grandfather and the rest of the family. Every visit was a new day for her because quite often she would not remember who we were. It was especially hard on my grandfather. So many years together and yet she didn't recognize him. It was always the same when her memory was gone, "Hi, it's nice to meet you." Then you would tell her all about yourself and if you were really lucky, she just might remember a tiny detail. Then a sparkle would come into her eyes as she processed that memory, and for a few short moments she would come alive again and you might carry on a short conversation. The memory would then fade and confusion and sometimes fear, would take its place as Grandma tried to figure out why a stranger was in her room. I know if there was a way to take that disease into his own mind and spare her, my grandfather would have. I can only imagine how hard and disappointing it must have been to look at the one you gave your life to and not have her recognize who you were, and at times even be afraid of you.

When you lose someone you love, it leaves a hole in your heart that mends slowly; but to watch your partner go through this terrible disease is like thrusting a fist into your chest and leaving the hole open. It drains the life from you and leaves you longing for yesterdays instead of tomorrows. It breaks your heart over and over again. A few years later, some of my aunts suffered from Alzheimer's and as I am writing this, one is still fighting it. Every time we go to see her it's always "Hi, it's nice to meet you." It is such a terrible disease that robs you of the most precious thing you have - your memory.

A Moment in Her Memory
Alzheimer's

"Good Morning" I said as I walked in her room
And a big smile lit up on her face
You see a visitor's welcome in her little world
It's so often a sad, lonely place

Her warm smile was friendly, but a tad bit confused
I could see that lost look in her eyes
For she wasn't quite sure if I should be there
Was I someone she should recognize

"Nice to meet you" she said as I neared her bed
And she stuck out her hand to shake mine
Too familiar I thought as I reached out for hers
We've done this over three hundred times

A beautiful woman, only seventy-four
Whose wrinkles add warmth to her face
But a mental confusion that twists up her mind
Is the reason she's here in this place

Her memory is clear for a moment some days
But too often it goes like the wind
Where it lingers somewhere just out of reach
Though she prays it will come back again

Alzheimer's is strange and so misunderstood
So cruel is the game that it plays
When it dangles a memory just out of reach
And taunts you the rest of your days

"Good Morning" he says as he enters the room
"You're looking quite lovely today"
That warm pretty smile again lights up her face
"Why thank you sir" I hear her say

I see that same hopeful look in his eyes
As he pulls his chair close to her side
She draws back when he tries to peck her on the cheek
And I feel his heart break as he sighs

He was hoping her memory was clearer today
And remembers the years they had shared
And he prays to his Lord to give it to him
So that his sweet bride may then be spared

He picks up her Bible and softly he reads
And she gladly lends him her ear
He's hoping today that God's word mends her mind
Like he's hoped every day for a year

As she drifts off to sleep he still stays by her side
He can't bear to leave her alone
He bends and gives her that peck on her cheek
And he takes her hand in his own

He closes his eyes and he goes back in time
To when he wore a younger man's clothes
And the pretty young lady that fancied him so
Would be the young wife he had chose

For fifty-four years every night at the door
She would greet her husband with a kiss
The plans that they had to grow old together
Should never have ended like this

So few are the times that she knows who he is
So few of her memories remain
The only comfort he finds in this plague of her mind
Is that she's not in any pain

He sees her confusion is taxing her so
And wished God would end it today
Then he asks for forgiveness and curses himself
All because he was thinking that way

He wishes time could just stop in its tracks
The next time her memory is clear
And if the Lord chose, he could take them both
As he embraced everything he holds dear

To hold her in his arms and share one more kiss
Would be a fair price for his life
And nothing could mean any more to him
Then to end life together with his wife

A moment of clarity, is that too much to ask
Just one precious moment in time
He just needs to know that she knows who he is
That he still has a place in her mind

But fate wouldn't have it, at least not today
For this day had come to an end
And I had to go tell him that he had to leave
Tomorrow he could see her again

"Do you think more pictures would help her?" he asks
"Or have the grandchildren come by?
I don't want to lose her, she's all that I have
Is there something else we can try?"

But her memory stayed hidden, like a hare in the briars
When a hunting coyote is near
For not once today did she know who he was
And that was the worst of his fears

He often wonders why God plagues the gentle
He struggles sometimes to believe
Why not the evil ones, unlike his sweet wife
Who wore her heart on her sleeve

As he picked up his jacket and readied to leave
I saw tears welling up in his eyes
He wanted to show her his love with a kiss
But instead softly whispered goodbye

She says, "It was so nice to meet you kind sir
You're welcome back here any time"
He says, "I just might take you up on that ma'am
But the pleasure has truly been mine"

The Big C

This tale is not a happy one
It often makes me cry
This is a story plagued with loss
For it's how my heroes died
I was only six-years-old
When Big C came to town
Set up camp in my father
Turned our smiles into frowns
I did not understand it
Ignorant because of youth
I searched only for answers
Someone to tell the truth
Too young I guess to fill me in
Or just to save me pain
But I longed to see him out of bed
To run, to play again

God blessed my father with great strength
For he hid from his family
The damage that Big C was doing
His pain, his agony
But I saw tears in my auntie's eyes
I heard my mother pray
I saw worry on my grandma's face
I saw this every day
Then I heard Granddad one day
Cussing out in the barn
"Damn it, if you want a soul
Take mine, he's done no harm"

So the birthday wish I wished that year
Was to take away his pain
But when my birthday came and went
The Big C still remained
So I went down to our family church
With pockets full of rocks
Intent on breaking stained glass there
To get my point across

They said that this was God's house
So I knew that he was there
I had to know why he refused
To answer all our prayers
I was hurling rocks with all my might
When someone grabbed my arm
And asked why I was so intent
On doing those windows harm
I said I needed God's attention
He said, "I think you got your way
Now run along and I'll forget
What you have done today"

I know that God was listening
For angels came that night
And fetched Dad's soul to heaven
Where he stepped into the light

Since then three uncles who I had
All on my mother's side
Each one's body was a host
Where Big C would reside
Each fought a valiant battle
Right up until the end
But Big C was much stronger
And took them in the end

And then my best friend's mother
Waged her own private war
And again when it was over
Big C had upped his score

My step-dad was a special man
He had a giant's heart
Big C arrived and took its hold
And tore his world apart
Such a gentle person
Who did no one any harm
The Big C finally took his life
And stole him from his farm

And then the gal just down the road
My dear wife's closest friend
So full of love and laughter
'Till Big C showed up again
That little lady fought so hard
We were all sure that she'd win
But she just wasn't strong enough
And Big C triumphed once again

I know it can be beaten
I've seen it done before
The trick is you must catch it
When it first comes knocking at your door
Big C once knocked our daughter down
When she was just a babe
But that young child was a fighter
And Big C didn't stay
Now every year she sees the doctor
As our world stops in its tracks
Until we hear those glorious words
"It still has not come back"

So many friends and loved ones
Where Big C changed their lives
Never for the better
Always pain and strife

And some day it may come for me
But I won't add to its score
I'll beat it down, throw it outside
Then turn and lock the door
I'm not the cold condemning kind
As far as I can tell
But damn this thing they call Big C
Damn it straight to hell

"You have to let go of the disease and hold on to
every moment of your life."

~ Farrah Faucet

The Bench

An old wooden bench sets on my front porch. Its back is weath-
ered and its armrests have been chewed by our dogs. It's not the
most comfortable piece of furniture on the porch; even the lawn
chairs give better support to a tired body. And it may not be the
best looking seat out there, but it's there for a reason.

It is a very significant piece of furniture. It sits next to my front
door like an old dog waiting for its master. The bench came
from my mother and step-father's farm where it sat next to their
front door. There on that bench, my step-father would take off
his boots after a long day in the orchards and rest for a brief mo-
ment before going into his house.

The bench came home with me when my mother moved into a
condo in town and there was no place to keep it. I gladly put it
near my door where it will continue to set as long as it holds up.
I placed it underneath a feeder and the hummingbirds drink only
a couple feet away as if they know as long as we're on that
bench, they are safe. This bench has become part of the porch
and I use it often when no one is around. It's a place I like to be
when I am alone. It beckons me as if to say, "Come sit and I'll
take you down memory lane." I do, and it does. I am often teary
eyed when I get up, and truth be told, that's one of the reasons I
often sit by myself. I've sat there with my wife and have been
just as comfortable, yet I didn't drift back like when I'm alone.
Don't get me wrong, I like sitting with her and I know that's
how Mitchell would like it—shared with someone we love. One
time as we sat on the bench together, one of our dogs jumped up
on my lap and down we went. The bench broke apart into sev-
eral pieces and we were on the floor with a surprised hound on
top of us. I took the bench to my shop and with a little glue,
some screws, and wire strapping, I managed to fix it so it could
once again set beside our door like a sentinel or old friend wait-
ing for us to come sit and remove our boots.

I've sat there before and wondered just how much that old bench has seen over the years—all the friends and family who passed by and the many strangers who were welcomed into the doorway. If only it could talk, what stories it could tell. I also wondered if it had feelings, how it must have felt that last week of my step-father's life as countless friends and loved ones passed by with worried faces and teary eyes. Did it know when I rushed by with pastor in tow, that Mitchell had passed away only seconds before and it would never again feel his warmth or weight as he removed his shoes.

I don't expect my dogs to understand when I scold them for gnawing on its arm rests. To them it's just a few pieces of weathered wood. And I guess my kids are not yet at a place where they can understand why I yell at them not to horse around on the porch or to take it somewhere else far away from the bench. "It's just a chair" they've told me. No, it's more than a chair. Someday they'll understand when I pass away. I can only hope that one of my possessions will bring them as much joy as this old bench does to me. May having it near bring them as much warmth and comfort as possible in my absence. With a new coat of paint the bench might look new again, but there would still be something missing. I know what that is, and I miss him too.

Respect

Sylvester Stallone said these words in his movie Rambo Two: "What do I want? I'll tell you what I want; I want what every soldier that ever fought for our country wants. I want our country to love us like we love our country."

Just words from a movie you say, just words. They may be just movie lines to most people, but they are thoughts that go through most Veteran's minds over and over again because we don't treat our soldiers as well as we should. They risk their lives so we can continue to live in a free country and enjoy a type of freedom no other country in the world enjoys. I believe every soldier coming home from a war deserves a heroes' welcome, but so many times there is no one at the gate to greet them. The VFWs and American Legion do an awesome job of going to the airports and greeting returning soldiers because many of them came home to empty gates or angry mobs of people themselves. They know how important it is to be welcomed home and what it means to a soldier. I hope the following pages at least make you stop for a moment and think about the sacrifices so many young men and women made to allow us these liberties. Perhaps if some of the following lines move you, you might, the next time you see a soldier, stick your hand out and say, "Thank you" or "We appreciate what you do." And who knows, you just might make their day a little brighter.

"We have enjoyed so much freedom for so long that we are perhaps in danger of forgetting how much blood it cost to establish the *Bill of Rights*."
~ Felix Frankfurter, Supreme Court Justice

"How little do my countrymen know what precious blessings they are in possession of, and which no other people on earth enjoy."
~ Thomas Jefferson

Old Glory Never Runs

Above a nation strong and free
A flag of freedom waves
It's also clutched in mother's hand
As her child's placed in a grave

A gift to each to let them know
Their deaths were not in vain
A piece of cloth transformed by heart
And love and sweat and pain

To soldiers who bravely gave their all
She's more than just a rag
She stands for God and country
And families of which they bragged

Though soaked with tears and brave men's blood
And bleached beneath the sun
She still flies high to tell the world
These colors never run

She was carried far from home
Across the raging seas
To help those who were trod upon
So they too could be free

She was carried in the trenches
And torn by jungle thorns
And drenched in ocean waters
Yet she still came back for more

She was carried up a thousand hills
And sometimes pushed back down
Only to fight back up again
And she never touched the ground

She flies above a nation free
Hard earned with guts and gun
To tell all who pose threat to us
These colors never run

She stands for peace and freedom
She stands for you and me
She represents a nation strong
There's no place I'd rather be

Her blue stands for the skies above
Where God has blessed the land
A star for every state of hers
United they all stand

The red is for the blood t'was shed
To keep her people free
And white is for each soldier's dreams
Of what they hoped to be

A symbol of a nation strong
She stands for all that's good
Where freedom is embraced by all
And peace and brotherhood

Yet, just lately we were tested
And for a moment stunned
But then we raised her up to prove
These colors never run

Again across the seas she's called
To restore a nation's rights
Unselfish and at risk of life
Again our soldiers fight

For they have tasted freedom
The only way to live
To bring that to other nations
Their lives they chose to give

The bravest men and women
Sons and daughters of us all
Risk life and limb unselfishly
As they answer freedom's call

So as you tuck your child in bed
Recall their sacrifice
So that we live free of tyranny
It's them who pay the price

They're heroes in a stranger's land
Danger wherever they roam
So say a prayer that each one there
Finds their way safely home

And thank the Lord for each of them
As they pick up their gun
And prove to those unjustly souls
These colors never run

Remember

Boot camp brought them together
Just boys still wet behind the ears
Strangers who pulled together
To help quell each other's fears

Their future held uncertainties
Things no man should have to face
They'd risk life and limb to save
Strangers in some ungodly place

Each would gladly risk his life
So a comrade wouldn't fall
For each one had the other's back
Trust, the unwritten law

They learned to band together
They fought to be the best
So when the Day of Judgment came
They'd surely pass the test

For war is such an empty place
Packed full of pain and strife
Where the order of the day is death
To live, you take a life

When you share a foxhole with a man
You can't help but wear his pain
You bare your souls, you share your hearts
You start to think the same

The story of your life is bared
Its pages stained with blood and sweat
From the soldiers who you've grown to love
And those you've never met

Like when Willy got his Dear John note
Each felt his heartache too
And the emptiness inside a man
That drains the life from you

When Gunny got that somber note
That said his father died
No one teased or put him down
Because the grown man cried

They all would miss letters from home
Signed by his father's hand
That told how proud he was of them
Because they took a stand

As Gunny read those letters
It brightened up their hell
So when his teardrops finally came
Their eyes were moist as well

When Harry's leg took sniper fire
That shattered all the bone
They felt his pain then thanked the Lord
Because now he could go home

Where he could see his newborn son
And hold him in his arms
And maybe live a normal life
Free from a sniper's harm

Oakie, he loved his country
And had no family left back home
He held Old Glory like a photograph
Each time he felt alone

Red, white, and blue, his saving grace
That filled him up with pride
Replaced the hollow feeling
That tore him up inside

Then one day he found his purpose
And with a smile upon his face
Threw himself across a hand grenade
That was their saving grace

For seven soldiers walked away
And bid a friend farewell
Content to know a comrade found
His own way out of hell

They battle on like heroes do
Until their tour is through
And fight to keep those freedoms
Bestowed on me and you

And when their tours are over
And they return back to the states
Why isn't everyone lined up
To meet them at the gates

Is a thank you too much to ask of us
For all their sacrifice
Or just to say we're proud of them
Because they paid the price

Do you know how many lives were lost
Through all the battles fought
Protecting rights that we abuse
Without a second thought

Freedom isn't free you know
So many soldiers fell
While we're at home enjoying life
They walk a living hell

They ask us for no payment
Our love alone is enough
And to know that we'll be here
Like they were there for us

To keep us free from tyranny
They do the things they do
So help support our soldiers friend
Because they're supporting you

And remember all of those who fell
Protecting all our rights
And ask the Lord to bless them
As you say your prayers tonight

And don't forget the wounded
Wounds of body and wounds of mind
And pray at home that they find peace
And not the hell they left behind

And pray for those who battle on
Wherever they may roam
That they might find peace tonight
And soon be coming home

God bless our soldiers
Those who served
Those who fell
Those who fight on

"Semper Fi" on the Homefront
Semper fi-delis

Collecting with the Red Cross
For our soldiers overseas
Everyone in that small town
Had given something up to me

'Till I came across a farmhouse
With fallen barn and shambled coops
And a dozen signs in an unmowed yard
That said, God bless our troops

Five flagpoles in her front yard
Four flew Old Glory high
The fifth was gold and crimson
The words read Semper Fi

Upon the porch an aging woman
Answered the door after I knocked
And when I asked for a donation
She seemed a little shocked

I thought she might be generous
Compared to others, might give more
But to my surprise she rolled her eyes
And turned and shut the door

The neighbor saw what happened
And he met me at the road
He said, "Now don't condemn her, son
She bears a heavy load"

You look a bit bewildered, son
So why don't you come with me
For back here on this shady knoll
There is something you should see

A sign that read beneath these oaks
Lay the graves of four brave men
To keep us free from tyranny
They fought tough to the end

Four wooden crosses stood there
A plaque on every one
Each bore a different title
Father, brother, husband, son

He said each cross has a story, son
A story you should hear
So sit down on this grieving bench
And let me bend your ear

Her father stormed the beach at Normandy
The day he lost his life
And gave it up protecting freedom
For his children and his wife

Korea is where her brother fell
Across a live grenade
And seven soldiers walked away
To fight another day

Her husband died in Vietnam
His grave lay empty 'neath that stone
He gave his life to save his men
And never did come home

On the blistering sands of Iraq fell
The only son she ever bore
As he saved a young child's life
That fell victim to that war

So please don't sit in judgment, son
And condemn in any way
For she wears their pains like an overcoat
On a cold and windy day

Her men's deaths have stained the pages
Of the story of her life
And stole her right to be a daughter
A sister, mother, and a wife

Semper Fi means always faithful, son
And I'd say she's done her part
So don't mistake her coldness
For the love of country in her heart

As I made my way back to the street
She was standing at the gate
In her hand she held four dollars
And had a warm smile on her face

I said, "You keep your money ma'am"
As teardrops filled my eyes
Then she took my hand and kissed my cheek
And whispered, "Semper Fi"

And now as I go door-to-door
To make collection calls
I'll remember on the home front too
All gave some, and some gave all

"The only necessary for the triumph of evil is for good men to stand by and do nothing."   ~ Edmond Burke

"It is easy to take liberty for granted when you have never had it taken from you."   ~ Dick Cheney

Coming Home

The flight was finally over
Our plane had just touched down
As soon as I was off those stairs
I kissed that hallowed ground

Glad to be back in the states
Me and my three best friends
Our tour was finally over
We were civilians once again

I was picking up my luggage
When a man walked up to me
And said "Are you just back from Iraq
Where you had no right to be"

He caught me unexpected
Though I knew this day would come
Our veterans caught the same flack
When they came back from Nam

I said, "Well, you are right sir
But you must not understand
What those poor souls were going through
Killed and tortured by Saddam"

Let's go talk over there, sir
My friends are much too near
The arguments you're making
I wish them not to hear

You see they didn't falter
When they were called to war
They said it was their duty
Just another nasty chore

They went to help a country
Whose people were not free
Where evil reigned and slaughtered
Any chance of liberty

They went to help people
Who were robbed and raped and slain
Their bodies by the thousands
Were dumped in open graves

The bodies weren't just soldiers
There were women and children too
Just innocent civilians
They were a lot like you

If evil came to your town
And slaughtered everyone
Wouldn't you be on your knees
Praying someone would come

These men answered their prayers
They did not hesitate
They could have just done nothing
Left those people to their fate

But evil cannot flourish
When good men answer their hail
Good always triumphs evil
And freedom will prevail

Yet freedom isn't free, sir
Lives surely will be lost
These men knew those risks
And were willing to pay the cost

They're heroes in my book, sir
So don't you talk them down
They gave their all for strangers
When no one else dared come around

What have you done today, sir
To pay for freedom's price
Have you even thought about it
How your life is so damn nice

Have you ever thanked a veteran
For taking up a stand
Or do you just condemn them
For what you don't understand

He stood there for a moment
The cat had got his tongue
But stupid folks say stupid things
I knew more words would come

He asked, "If there are four of you
Where are the other three
That you say fought like heroes
To set people free"

Well sir, they're laying over there
Each in a body bag
Inside those metal coffins
Draped with a U.S. flag

You see they gave their all, sir
Because freedom isn't free
Those rights you take for granted
Mean so much more to me

I suggest you back away sir
For now you've got my dander up
And you haven't got an inkling
As to what those men gave up

I am forever faithful
To my brothers of the corps
And to my God and country
In times of peace and war

So don't you talk them down, sir
Because of men like them you're free
And if you disrespect them
You walk the fighting side of me

I will defend their honor
As long as I draw breath
Protecting people just like you
Was how they met their death

People that don't appreciate
What our armed forces do
Protecting all the freedoms
Bestowed on men like you

So go ahead, enjoy your day
And kiss your kids tonight
And if you have a conscience
Say a prayer for those who fight

And if that's not what you believe
Well, I guess that is your choice
Another freedom that has cost
The lives of girls and boys

I hope you understand, sir
And I hope the day won't come
When war breaks out again and
Uncle Sam calls out your son

God Bless Our Soldiers.
Thank them when you see them.

"You'll never know how much your freedom has
cost my generation. I hope that you don't squander it."
~ John Quincy Adams

They say that man is the most intelligent creature on
Earth. If this is so, why are we the only creatures who
declare war on ourselves? Intelligent life?
I think not.

~ Author

Like a Picture in a Broken Frame

Middle aged and lonely, nobody seems to give a damn
Just another messed up Veteran, a souvenir of Vietnam

Who had hoped he could forget and leave the war behind
He tries so hard to shut it out, but it penetrates his mind

At night he dreams in color, in camouflages and blood red
As sounds of screams and gunfire echo through his head

He wakes up in a cold sweat, pulling at his hair
Of all the places in the world, why do his dreams go there

He's back there on the war front, bullets flying overhead
He's trying to reach a wounded buddy, so many soldiers dead

Confusion's hanging overhead and discomfort fills the air
Death hovers like a vulture, fear is spreading everywhere

Napalm in the distant has the horizon glowing red
Choppers flying back and forth as they taxi out the dead

The day is hot and bloody, sulfur and flesh are all he smells
Screams of pain surround him like he's at the gates of hell

He doesn't care about himself, a comrade needs a helping hand
If he can't get him out of here, he'll die there in the sand

So he stands and empties out his gun, and throws his last grenade
Then dashes through the gunfire to where his buddy lays

He grabs him by his backpack, dragging him out of harm's way
Only ten more yards to safety, it seems such a long, long way

His legs and side are aching now, but the foxhole is so near
It takes everything he's got, but he gets his buddy clear

Tending to that soldier's wounds, he doesn't notice all the blood
That's soaking through his camo, dripping down into the mud

In all of the excitement, he never realized
A bullet went in through his gut and came back out his side

Another blew apart his knee and shattered all the bone
This happened thirty years ago, that's why they sent him home

But he'll relive it every night, until his dying day
His penance for our freedom, he never should have paid

He feels just like a picture hanging in a broken frame
Hanging on for all he's worth but every day's the same

Like a cracked and faded photograph, he hangs out all alone
Forgotten in some dingy room in some disabled veteran home

They said he was a hero, but he never felt that way
His comrades would've done the same, if he were in harm's way

He was honored for a moment, the length of a float ride
But when the parade was over, they cast him to the side

His meager veteran's benefits will hardly pay his bills
And anything that might be left is used to buy more pills

To make him sleep, to fight his pain, to help him clear his head
For some days he can hardly cope and wishes he were dead

He's not the only one like this, there's a hundred thousand more
Someone's son or daughter who fell victim to a war

They give their all protecting rights we don't appreciate
Those rights we take for granted, back here in the United States

Heroes In Plaid

We plucked them from their childhood, forced each to be a man
Stuck them in a gun fight, shoved a weapon in their hand

Told them to kill or be killed, fighting someone else's war
Take a hill, then give it back, what are they dying for

Washington won't let them win, it's all bureaucratic crap
Politics and war don't mix, it gets our soldiers trapped

Trapped between the enemy and politicians here at home
Who don't care about their welfare, just agendas of their own

We told them to fight like heroes, make America be proud
When they came home we shunned them, lost them in the crowd

Behind this country and its leaders, I'll do my duty and I'll stand
But I can't always say I'm proud, to be American

Sometimes it's damn embarrassing what our so-called leaders do
Interested more in oil than folks like me and you

And to forget about our soldiers, that just does not seem right
Where would we all be today, if they chose not to fight

We wouldn't have the freedoms that we enjoy still today
So help a veteran, brother, help him enjoy his day

Tell him that you're proud of him, tell him you understand
Then if you have a heart at all, give him a helping hand

He doesn't want a handout; he just wants to know you care
And that there are some thankful folks, who understand out there

"Liberty has never come from the government. Liberty has
always come from the subjects of it. The history of liberty is a
history of resistance."
~ Benjamin Franklin

The Wall

I went and saw the Wall today
A visit long, long overdue
I wish now I'd seen it sooner
Then gone back a time or two

I wasn't sure what to expect
It's just a long black stone
Too ignorant to understand
Each name was flesh and bone

As I got nearer, I could see
So many soldier's names
Arranged in years they gave their lives
The years that they were slain

So many men and women's names
Were carved into that Wall
Unselfish souls who gave their lives
To answer freedom's call

The names were grouped by dates
Not red, yellow, black, or white
Because color doesn't matter
When you're in a firefight

They all were brothers in the field
Each one of them bled red
Unlike us, they flushed those prejudices
Trapped inside their heads

You see, race doesn't matter
When fighting for a cause
Red and black and white men
Together they were lost

I saw older people kneeling
Tracing names upon that Wall
And as each stood to walk away
I saw their teardrops fall

I saw children running, laughing
Having fun without a care
The very reason each one of those names
Was clearly printed there

And then it started sinking in
The vastness of it all
For every name upon that Wall
Meant a good man had to fall

I started reading one by one
The names etched in that stone
Each a son or daughter
Who never made it home

Each left a grieving parent
A sibling, child, or wife
Because they were protecting
Someone else's way of life

As I reached out to touch the Wall
Expecting damp, cold stone
What happened then enlightened me
Yet chilled me to the bone

I felt a pulse each time I reached
And touched a soldier's name
That black stone had a heartbeat
And I felt each soldier's pain

That Wall was reaching out to me
Its message clear and loud
Don't squander all your freedoms
Stand tall and make us proud

Like our forefathers before us
We fought to make things right
Don't let our nation be oppressed
Pick up the cause and fight

Don't let our lives be lost in vain
Please keep our memory clear
Uphold our Constitution
That each of us held dear

And then I looked into the books
That they had placed nearby
I saw soldiers from my hometown
And I began to cry

Because I could remember
Back to when I was a lad
The soldiers going off to war
Brothers of friend's I had

That's when it really hit me
And drove me to my knees
Finally it was personal
I saw the forest for the trees

It wasn't just a piece of stone
A monument or plaque
It was a living testament
To each name etched in black

It stood to say these young souls gave
Their lives to keep us free
So that we may live a life
Free of tyranny

So I implore and beg you
To go and see the Wall
And read the names of heroes there
That answered freedom's call

Because freedom isn't free, you know
Lives surely will be lost
So say a prayer they rest in peace
All those who paid that cost

The Visit

I was fishing the Big Manistee one morning and there were very few on the river because it was so cold. I had a decent stretch to myself and although I passed a couple guys on the way in, there were no fishermen in sight. The steelhead were holding tight, if they were there at all, and I hadn't had a bite all morning. My mind was drifting off to past trips to this place and how the action was often slow when the water was this cold. The thought of a warm cabin was sounding pretty good. I told myself I would make a few more casts and then call it a morning when I saw his reflection in the water and I smiled. He smiled back and not thinking, I turned to look at him. There was no one there and when I turned back to see his reflection, there was nothing but ripples rolling across the caramel-colored water. I don't know why I turned to look. I knew it couldn't be him; he passed away several months ago. Just wishful thinking, I guess, for I longed to see his face again and for a short time share a small stretch of river with a true friend.

You meet a lot of people in your life and very few of them ever materialize into true friends. He was one of those who are so few and far between, the kind with whom you can share what's on your mind or in your heart. If you bare your soul, you know it will never come back and bite you in the behind because they respect and except you for who you are, not who they wished you were.

He loved to fish and we've shared this stretch of river in the past. The fishing wasn't always the greatest, but the company was a welcome joy and always left you walking away from the day feeling better for just sharing time with him.

I don't believe in ghosts, but I do believe in what my sister-in-law refers to as "visits"—where a lost loved one appears for a brief second, or you feel their presence or get a whiff of their cologne or perfume. That's what this was, a visit. It felt as though he was sitting there on the bank, watching over my shoulder as I cast into the icy cold waters several more times to no avail. My mind drifted back to the last time we were here and what had and hadn't produced a strike. I dug through my vest and found an egg-sucking leech fly that he had given me and I tied it on to my line. On the second cast my line tightened and when I set the hook, a silver bullet exploded out of the water and tail-walked across the surface. She fought hard for a few minutes and then came quietly into my net. I carefully unhooked her and set her free to go lay her eggs and help to restock this awesome fishery. I felt a tear welling up in my eye and I went to sit on the bank for a moment to collect myself. I know where that fish came from. It was a gift from a friend, as was that reflection on the water just a few short minutes ago. It warmed me and made a cold, lonely morning on the river become a beautiful day. Any day on the river is better than a day at work, but shared with someone, even a memory or a "visit," is so much more pleasant.

A few weeks back an old friend walked up to me and asked, "Have I ever told you how much I appreciated our friendship? You are a special friend and I just wanted to let you know that."

He caught me unexpectedly and I was at a loss for words. I just mumbled, "I feel the same way." Then I quickly looked around to make sure no one had heard us. He smiled and walked away and it really got me thinking about my life. If I were to leave this earth today, would friends and family know how much I valued their companionship and their love? I wasn't so sure, and it ate at me for the longest time. I had remembered a letter about flowers for the living that a friend had put in the newspaper over twenty years ago. She said she had attended a funeral where there were so many flowers from friends and families with little cards all saying how much they cared. She wondered if those people who sent the flowers talked about how much they cared while the person was still alive. My friend had just gotten out of the hospital where she received many flowers; yet it was the visits from friends and the conversations they had that meant so much more. "Flowers for the living" was what she called those visits. They were "good for the heart." Several friends had told her how much she meant to them and she believed those shared feelings were stronger than any medication she was on.

I thought about that while I was sitting on the bank and wondered if my buddy ever knew how much I valued our friendship. I know I never came out and told him. It's not a manly thing to do, or is it? I don't think any less of that friend who told me that. In fact I value our friendship even more now that I know. We had plenty of conversations between us, my buddy and I. We knew we would be there for each other if one needed a helping hand, but I never came out and said how important his friendship was. I felt I needed to tell him and I sat there on the bank and did just that. Then I packed up and headed home. On the way I called his wife to see how she was doing. We shared a few tears across the airwaves and as we were about to hang up she said, "You know he really valued your friendship. You meant a lot to him."

I hung up thinking: *He just told me. Why couldn't I have had the guts to tell him face-to-face?* I can only hope he knew how special he was.

[59]

Prelude
to
Lost Loved One

Florence

A few years back I had a family friend who was very ill and we knew her time was short. She had been a friend of the family long before I was born and after my father passed away, she often took care of us so my mother could work. She was a beautiful person from the inside out, with a warm heart who always worried about us. She was a blessing to our family and to me as well, and she was always reassuring me that it was only going to get better. The last time I saw her she knew that she was failing, yet she was still such a happy person. She told us that night that she was ready to go home and be with her husband who had passed away years before. She said God had a place for her and she was ready. When she saw the tears in my eyes she told me not to worry and that I would see that everything would be okay.

A couple nights later I was walking up from the barn. It was about 10:30 in the evening and I was looking up at the beautiful night sky. I saw a shooting star and it seemed to slow, and then as it neared another star, it seemed to stop. I went to bed that night not sure if I really saw anything at all because it was just so strange. My eyes are not what they used to be and for all I knew, it could have been a satellite. The other stars in the sky that night seemed to react as it passed by, but I just figured it was my imagination.

The next morning I got a phone call that said our dear friend had passed away, and in an instant, I realized what I had seen. It was her way of telling me that everything would be okay. We had lost an angel, but she had gone home and joined her husband in the place God had made for her. May God bless you Florence, like God blessed us with your presence when you were here on Earth.

Lost Loved One

Last night while walking in my yard
Gazing up at heaven's light
I saw a shooting star go by
Then stop there in the night
It twinkled for a second
And then when on its way
I thought it strange to move like that
And why it didn't stay
As it moved about the heavens
Others twinkled as it passed
And then it straightened out
And made a bee-line path
This star off in the distance
It started glowing bright
It seemed this one that's moving
Was attracted to its light
It shot just like an arrow
A collision I had feared
It moved so straight and swiftly
Then slowed just as it neared
Those two stars came together
Then hung as one there in the night
I marveled at their beauty
And how they shone so bright
Then I awoke the next morning
Still puzzled by the show
For a lack of explanation
I guessed I saw a UFO
I never paid attention
To the beauty up above
Or how God gave us the heavens
As a token of his love
Then I got the phone call
That said a loved one passed away
And everything was clearer
Here in the light of day

That star I saw go by last night
With a light that shone of gold
It was that loved one passing by
As God gathered up her soul
And when it stopped and twinkled
There in the clear night sky
It was her way of reassuring me
And then to say goodbye
Those other stars that twinkled
Were souls that passed before
Welcoming her into their arms
As she passed through heaven's door
And that star which shone so brightly
And guided our loved one's flight
It was the Lord and Savior
As He welcomed home His child
Now they're both there together
Their journey now is through
They're up there with the others
Watching over me and you
I know not to be afraid
For angels fill the sky
And they will guide us safely home
When it comes our time to die
Such a kind and gentle person
With so much love to share
I know you know you left behind
So many folks who care
I know you will be dearly missed
No one can fill your shoes
For you have touched so many lives
But now God has plans for you
We know you will not be lonely
For heaven's full of friends
Those others who we dearly loved
Who reached their journey's end
Tell them like you, we miss them

And let them know we care
And along with yours at our journey's end
Their embraces we will share
This earth has lost an angel
But our loss is heaven's gain
And we know God will embrace you
'Till we see your face again
Although you may be out of sight
And our paths may seem to part
You'll always be a piece of us
You're forever in our hearts

The Rack

There he stood next to that old station wagon dressed in his red wool hunting outfit with a smile as big as Texas across his face. His right hand lay across the eight-point rack of the buck he had strapped atop that car. I remembered being in awe and excited when he asked us boys to help him hang it. I gathered up my friends to show off the buck my father had shot. I was so proud to be his son, and so proud of that buck. I wish I could have known that would be the last deer my father would ever hunt. Cancer took hold of him and he never got back to the woods before the Lord took him home.

I wish I had the sense to keep that rack as a memorial to one of the greatest men I ever knew. I would like to have been able to give to my youngest brother so it could adorn his wall. On his wall are many trophies, as there are on the walls of my other brothers and mine. All these racks represent special hunts we like to remember. None would be as special as that last rack of our father's.

I would chose to have it hang on my youngest brother's wall because he never got to know our father. He was just a baby when Dad passed away, but that didn't stop him from inheriting a love for the hunt, or for the whitetail that now is a large part of his life. This love of hunting is present in all of us. My wife, however, would say it's more of an obsession than a pastime.

I have a feeling that if this rack were hanging on his wall, it would gather the least dust and be shown off the most. Although it is far from the biggest, it would mean the most. If it were in my house, it too would be treated like the most treasured piece of art. I would have been torn as to where to keep it though. Should it go in the safe to guard it from vandals and thieves, to remain secure from fire; or should it hang on the wall where it could be shown off because it represents so much. It would be my greatest possession. As I took it in my hands and ran my fingers across its tines, it would draw from my memory an image of Dad as clear as if he were standing in front of me at that very moment, smiling ear to ear, full of life and aglow with that feeling that a day in the woods so often leaves you with. He was a lover of life and a giver of love, a joy to be around. He was as comfortable in the out-of-doors as he was in his own skin, and that he passed down to us. We will be forever grateful.

There are many other articles within my house that represent great men in my life. There is a set of antlers my grandfather got off the moose he shot back in 1939, and a deer-foot gun rack that holds a homemade muzzleloader my wife's grandfather used to own, made by his grandfather. There's a 'No Hunting' sign that used to hang in the swamp where my Uncle Gayle used to take me. This swamp was bought by the state, but I still hunt there to this day. And an old yellow sweater hangs in my closet that my Uncle Frank used to wear around deer camp. I sometimes slip it on when I want to go down memory lane, or when I need a little luck in the deer woods. A diary my Uncle Chuck used to carry into battle is on my bookshelf. It keeps me on the straight and narrow and reminds me that deer camp is not really about shooting deer. There's a water can that tells the tale of a deer camp that began some sixty years ago and still goes on each November with the same bloodline, just some newer faces. A picture hangs on my wall of my father's deer camp where my father, grandfather, Uncle Jack, and my first boss are all raising their beers to toast the good life. These and other articles lay about my house to pay tribute to the men I most admired in my life. These were great men who I looked up to and had the great fortune to share hunts with. These were men I could only aspire to be like, for they were my heroes.

Yes, my heroes wore Woolrich and dressed in red plaid.

The Wedding

The weather this day was picture perfect—warm and clear with a gentle breeze that was just enough to keep us refreshed. We had been kayaking before noon and couldn't have asked for a more beautiful morning. Now it was about four in the afternoon and we were trying to wind our way across the state to a wedding ceremony. I knew I was in for trouble when my mother said we didn't need the directions from the internet. She was in the backseat giving directions and I was getting a bit uptight because I hate to be late. I knew if we followed the printed directions we would get there quicker, but Mom had them in the backseat and wouldn't give them up. "Turn here," she said, and I barked back that I knew this road was not in the directions.

She said, "You should have turned back there, but it doesn't matter because I know a road up ahead that will take us straight across the state."

"Straight across?" I asked.

"Straight as an arrow" she replied "just up ahead a mile."

After about seven miles or so I began to question her directions; but she insisted she knew the way. When the road came to an end a few miles later, she said, "See, just like I said. Turn here. This road is straight and we can make good time."

After about two hundred feet, I made a ninety degree turn. For the next thirty or so miles I had no idea which direction I was headed. Every quarter mile, I was turning ninety-degrees again and beginning to get motion sickness. The sun was in my eyes on the left, on the right, in my rearview mirror, and then back in my eyes again at least once every mile we traveled. When we got to the end of that road I asked which direction I turned and Mom replied, "It doesn't matter, whichever way you want. Let's go left. No, let's go right."

I heard my wife and kids giggle and I thought I must have heard her wrong. "What way?" I asked. "Fine," she said, "Go left."

More giggling came from the peanut gallery which was surely enjoying the ride more than me. So I turned left. "When this road ends, we turn right, go through town, and then just another mile and we are there." were the next directions given. And I'll be darned if they weren't right.

As we turned off the main road into the resort where the ceremony was, an old familiar rock song invaded my head *It's a Great Day for a White Wedding*. I hadn't heard it in thirty years but the words seemed to fit the occasion. At least those words; I couldn't remember any more of them. And then, as we turned into the parking lot, I saw a few familiar trucks and the noise in my head quickly changed to the lyrics of a country tune: *I ain't as good as I once was, but I'm as good once as I ever was*. A smile formed on my face at the same time as a tear formed in my eye. That was my cousin Jim's favorite song. I was remembering him at deer camp, standing outside the tents and singing it at the top of his lungs. And today was his daughter's wedding. It was a day he hoped would come because he very much approved of the man she was about to marry. It was something we had talked about when the camp was quiet and just the two of us would sit and talk about that which was important in our lives. His daughter was very much an important part of Jim's life and he often would say "I wish he would hurry up and ask her. They seem so right for each other." He finally did, but Jim wasn't here to see it. He had passed away a year and a half ago and he couldn't be here today to see her make those vows, at least not in the physical sense that is. As the day played out, I felt more and more sure that he was there and he was watching. He must have been very proud.

The wedding was at Garland, a golf resort in upper Michigan, and as the crow flies, less than a dozen miles from our deer camp. That was the reason we were here, at this place, at this time. Jim's ashes had been spread at deer camp and his daughter wanted to be close to him on her very special day.

We quickly found our seats which were spread on the lawn under some shade trees. We sat among relatives and friends as the ceremony began. The groom made his way to the front and soon the wedding party was filing in. As they made their way down the aisle, I saw a picture near the altar with a candle burning next to it. It was a picture of Jim, and I felt my eyes again begin to tear up. The music started and we all turned to look at the bride. She was every bit as beautiful as her father had said she would be. Her mother had her by the arm and as she walked down the aisle, every eye was on her. I felt a bit guilty for a moment, guilt that I was witnessing this and he was unable to be here. And then, a warm breeze touched my face and I knew that he was watching. She was crying and I believe every eye in the crowd was wet with tears. If they weren't, I sure couldn't tell because mine were flowing like a river. There were tears of joy that day, mixed with those tears that come when you miss someone. Everyone in those chairs was missing Jim. We were all happy for the bride and wishing her the best, but we could see that she was hurting for her father. Many of us felt those same pangs she was feeling—the ones that tug at your heart and leave you feeling a little hollow inside.

As the ceremony went on, I listened to what the preacher was saying, but my mind was wandering back several years to when her father was bouncing her on his knee, and when she was helping her grandmother in the kitchen, and every year at deer camp when her father and I would sit next to each other and have our little talks. Sometimes we would meet for lunch in the swamp or take a ride in the truck and share the things that were dear to our hearts. Always, the subject was our children, and no doubt he was very proud of his. He talked about when she was power-lifting and working out. He joked about how she could probably whip any boy around, and that's why she didn't have a boyfriend; they were scared of her. "She might be tough, but she's twice as pretty," he would say. We both agreed he was right. He talked about her job and how he missed her not living at home. He talked about the boy she finally brought home to meet him. "He's a Yooper, but he doesn't hunt and he doesn't even have a truck. Don't you think that's strange?" Jim said. "But all in all, he's a pretty good kid." When I asked if he was good enough for his daughter, he said, "Nobody is good enough for my daughter, but I like him and I approve." I knew exactly where he was coming from, having daughters of my own.

Like a movie on fast forward, those memories were coming into my head. And then, as if someone reached up and hit pause, they stopped and we were standing next to the stream that runs through the swamp where we hunt. This was Jim's favorite place and where his ashes were about to be spread. We all stood next to the stream as his son poured his remains into the crystal clear waters that flowed through his favorite hunting grounds. His ashes seemed to float there for a moment as if they were saying goodbye, and then they made a circle in the small pool there in the stream as if to get one last glimpse of family before following the current downstream.

My mind snapped back to the present when I heard the preacher introduce the newlyweds. As they walked by, I again felt that warm breeze on my face. I felt his presence and I think it was his way of saying "See, I told you she'd be gorgeous." And she was. The bride and groom greeted their guests and when it came my turn, I gave her a big hug and told her how beautiful she looked. I wanted to say how proud her dad would have been, but I got choked up. I could see in her eyes she understood and no words needed to be shared. The groom said he would see me at deer camp and I felt a jolt of satisfaction flow through me.

As we made our way across the lawn to the reception hall, any doubts that her father was watching went by way of the wind when a young buck stepped out of the shadows and stood not thirty yards away as we all filed in. Perfect I thought; just perfect. I bet he had something to do with this beautiful weather too.

[69]

Seeing that young buck took me back to deer camp this last fall. On opening day I sat in the very same part of the swamp that Jim and I shared. I fell asleep around lunch time and was out for awhile when I heard a voice say "Dan, wake up. There's a buck." I opened my eyes expecting to see someone standing there. There was a buck at twenty yards, standing broadside. I picked up my rifle and filled my tag. The next morning I had to take my youngest son home, but I told my oldest son to sit in my blind and drop Jim's son off in his blind. As fate would have it, they couldn't find one of the blinds, so they sat together. A young buck came in and my son harvested his first deer with the help of his cousin, just like I had done over the years with Jim. I'm sure Jim had something to do with that too. The tradition lives on.

We got into the reception hall and there on the table was her late grandmother's peanut butter cake. "Awesome," I thought, "Grandma's here too." The reception was awesome and the food was great. We very much enjoyed it as we talked with relatives and once again agreed that we have to get together more on happy occasions like this instead of at funerals. As we got ready to leave, I went out to get the car to come back to pick up my family. I turned the key; the car started. The radio came on and what lyrics do you think I heard? You got it—*I ain't as good as I once was, but I'm as good once as I ever was.* Coincidence you say. I think not!

Corie,

Your wedding was perfect. Except for the fact that your dad wasn't there to walk you down the aisle, it was everything he would have wanted. The log buildings, the fact that it was outside, the location, and most of all, the fact that you married Matt. More than once, your dad said he wished Matt would hurry up and ask you because he knew that you two were right for each other. The words I have written reflect how your wedding played out for me. I thought it was in a perfect place, and when I saw that buck step out and stand there as we passed, I felt your father's presence like I so often feel our uncles and your grandfathers when I'm in the cedar swamps at camp. It's hard to explain, but when its cold or snowing and I think I should go back to camp, I'll suddenly feel a warm breath of air upon my face and I'm content to sit for several more hours, I know that although there are no other hunters around, I am not alone. That feeling is what carries me through the year and I so look forward to getting back there each fall. Like your Dad, I've come to realize that getting a deer has very little to do with our hunts being successful. Those swamps are special to all of us because we feel closest to those with whom we used to share camp. I feel closer to those who have passed on, and I just know they are watching over us. I look forward to sharing camp with Matt. Let him know he is always welcome.

You were every bit as beautiful a bride as your dad said you would be and I am sure he is very proud of you. Stay close to your family, enjoy your new life with Matt, and don't let weeds grow around your dreams. Go out and live them. That is what your dad would have wanted.

Love always,

Dan

Anyone Can Be a Father

When my son was just a baby, I took him to see my grand-mother who was ninety-three at the time. As I was leaving, she said, "Remember anyone can be a father, but a daddy takes a man. That child needs your time more than any monetary things. He needs to know he's loved." Six years later found me a single parent only getting to see my son on weekends. At the time, I thought I needed the overtime work provided and so part of those weekends with him, I would take him to a sitter and go into work. One morning, I overheard some kids teasing my son about not having a full-time dad. He defended me and then made up some stories about things we did. These were things I had said we would do but had never got around to. It was then that my grandmother's words echoed in my head and I realized my shortcomings as a father. I called into work and went out and told my son we were going to do some of those things right now. The smile on that little face reinforced my belief that my grandmother, God rest her soul, was a very, very wise woman.

My hope is that this poem makes a difference in some parent's life and they realize how important time with their children is.

Other words of wisdom from my Grandma Bachi:

"Eyes that never cry will never shine." She believed you needed to grieve and get passed it so your eyes would again sparkle with their memory.

"You can wake up in the morning and your roses can have thorns, or your thorns can have roses. The choice is yours." Choose a positive attitude; your thorns will all have roses and it will be a beautiful day.

Weekend Daddy

Another Friday night I picked him up
Like weekend daddy's do
As he came running down the drive
He yelled, "Daddy, I missed you"
He jumped up in my arms and asked
"Do you miss me too?"
So I kissed him on his head and said
"Yeah, Son, I surely do"
We climbed up in my old blue truck
Drove home to watch TV
He sat there on my lap awhile
Then fell asleep across my knee
As I looked down on my sleeping child
A question burned in me
In my quest to be a daddy
Am I all that I can be?
My grandma gave me some advice
When my son was just a babe
But before I fully understood
The Lord took her away
And now as I recall her final words
I still don't understand
She said anyone can be a father
But a daddy takes a man
Give them all you can while they are still young
Because a childhood never lasts
Children age so quickly now
This world turns so darn fast
It's not the child support you pay
Or the toys you keep on hand
But the love you give, the time you share
Is the true measure of a man

The next morning in the kitchen
As I fixed a bite to eat
I heard him fighting in the backyard

[73]

With the boys from down the street
I stood there by the screen door
To hear what they had to say
I heard, "He's just a weekend daddy
Who don't need you anyway
When you going to realize boy
Your daddy don't need you
And he only comes around when
He's got nothing else to do"
My son said, "Sticks and stones may break my bones
But words won't make me cry
'Cause my daddy says he loves me
And my daddy never lies
He just took me fishing
We got brand new fishing' poles
And we caught a bunch of big ones
At our secret fishing hole
Well then I walked over to the closet
And my eyes welled up with tears
As I looked down on those rods and reels
I hadn't used in years
My son was making stories up
Of things we'd never done
Those simple things in life
I should be sharing with my son
Well then I started thinking
What I thought the night before
How when it came to sharing time
I owed him so much more
And as I recalled my grandma's words
I began to understand
She said anyone can be a father
But a daddy takes a man

Give them all you can while they are still young
Because a childhood never lasts
Children age so quickly now
Their world turns so darn fast

It's not the child support you pay
Or the toys you keep on hand
But the love you give the time you share
Is the true measure of a man
My father died when I was young
So many things we couldn't do
Now all those things I missed in life
My son was missing too
All the hours of overtime I worked
To build this better home
Had robbed my son of childhood dreams
And left him all alone
So I called the boss and told him
"I won't be in today"
Went out into the yard and said
There's no more time to play
Son, I see your having lots of fun but
Now it's time to go
Because I hear they're catching big ones
At our secret fishing hole
All the overtime I worked
Could never take the place
Of the smile I saw that moment
Come across that young child's face
And as I recalled my grandma's words
I finally understand
Anyone can be a father
But a daddy takes a man

Give them all they need while they are still young
Because a childhood never lasts
Children age so quickly now
Their world turns so darn fast
It's not the child support you pay
Or the toys you keep on hand
But the love you give the time you share
Is the true measure of a man

Gordo T

The bags are packed, everything is loaded, and we are out the door. "Have you got everything?" A quick "yes" was given and then it's back in the door, back out again, and then back in again for one last thing. Another goodbye, a few more tears from my wife, and then we were in our cars.

My wife asked me if I was going to get all misty eyed when I left him all the way up there at school? I said I wouldn't get all emotional because we would see him in a couple months and it was no big deal. She said that I may not cry but she bet my eyes would get moist and my lip would turn up like she says it does when I get emotional or passionate about something. I told her she was crazy and that I didn't do that. She spouted out that I would see; and with that, we were off.

I noticed the letters "Gordo T" on the license plate of my son Gordon's car as he pulled out the drive. I pulled out behind him and would stare at that plate for the next 530 miles, the distance to Michigan Tech where he would be enlisting as a freshman.

The trip was pretty much straight up the interstate to the Mackinaw Bridge. We crossed over and we were in the U.P., and with a couple more turns and a lot of miles between, we were there. The route was simple and direct and the car made it with no detours or turn-offs other than a stop for gas. I can't say the same thing for my mind though because it wandered back and forth to several different places and a time zone that spanned the last eighteen years of my son's life. As the odometer clicked away the miles, I drifted back through the few short years of his life.

I remembered when he was born. He was in a hurry to come into the world and arrived three weeks early after his mother was involved in a car accident. I remember watching a heart monitor that was hooked up to his mother and seeing his heartbeat drop from over a hundred beats a minute to less than twenty. I ran out and grabbed a doctor and in a few short minutes she was rushed away to have a C-section. The umbilical cord had wrapped around his wrist and was closing off his circulation. So he was rushed into this world and now looking back, it seems he rushed through the last eighteen years.

I remember my grandma rocking him when he was just a few weeks old, saying "If everyone had one of these to come home to every night, there would be no crime in the streets."

I remember my grandfather holding him up months before he could walk trying to encourage him to take a few steps and telling me how he looked like my father did and how my father would be proud that he had his name.

I remembered waking up in the middle of the night to the smallest little sound and rushing into his bedroom just to see him sleeping peacefully. I recall his first birthday when he had more cake in his hair than on his plate.

I remember when my Stepfather Mitch first met my son and took a shine to him right off. They were best buddies from then on. Wherever Grandpa Mitch went, so did Gordon and HeyYou (the dog). Whether it was in the truck, on the tractor, or just for a walk, the three of them were inseparable.

At my mother and Mitch's farm, I remember when he and his best friend, HeyYou, were in the orchard stuffing down sweet cherries. Apparently he had one too many and came running in the house with his legs together on his way to the toilet yelling, "Grandma, I have ballerina." It didn't take long to realize that he was about to mess his pants.

When he was four, we were fishing on Mitch's farm and he asked my brother if he could use the rubber crayfish in his tackle-box. My brother laughed and put it on his line for him. By the time we were done fishing, he had three bass, a pike, and several large bluegills and sunfish. My brothers and my combined catch were far less than that.

On his fifth birthday, I was in Colorado hunting Elk and he reminded me for years that it was his worst birthday ever. I still feel bad about that to this day.

When he was five, I remember cooking his favorite dish for him—macaroni and cheese. I had my shirt off and was wearing shorts and he was looking at all my scars and asking me how I got them. I told him one was from a chain saw, a couple were from power saws, one from falling on a jagged rock, and a couple from burns and a few other things. I took the noodles off the stove and was draining them in the sink when I heard him yell. I turned around to see him yanking his hand off the burner. He ran over to me and we put his fingers in cold water. He pulled his fingers out and asked if he was going to have a scar. I told him no, that he was lucky this time. He then jumped up and ran over to the stove and put his hand on the burner again and yelled. He ran back to me and we put his fingers under water. I asked him why he did that and he said he wanted a scar like big boys have. I explained that he had one on his back where he had a mole removed and after a check in the mirror he thought he was pretty cool. "Now," he said, "all I need is hair in my ears like Grandpa."

I remember when he was five and I came out the door of my house to see him standing next to the neighbor girl, both with their pants down around their ankles. "What are you doing?" I yelled to him. "She doesn't know how to pee standing up, Dad, so I'm teaching her."

Memories were passing through my mind as quickly as the white lines were passing under my tires, and soon we were standing at my mother and Mitch's farm. Mitch lay there about to leave the world. He had fought a valiant battle, but the Lord was taking him to a better place. We were in the room when he drew his last breath, and Gordon just looked on and no tears fell. I, on the other hand, was crying like a baby. It was three hours later up in a room with just my wife and I when that dam finally broke and Gordon's tears rushed out. He would miss his best friend and Grandpa and of course does to this day.

His grandfather left him a 30-06 to hunt deer and I remember sitting in a blind with him, looking over his shoulder and down his barrel at a fat, little spike buck. "Shoot," I whispered in his ear. "I can't see it dad," he said; and he never did shoot. I think he was content just watching it feed and wished it no harm, so I never raised my rifle.

The last couple years, I remember Gordon's teachers telling me what a joy he was in school and how I must be so proud. I was, and I am. I recall his junior year when he was taking a girl to the prom. I called him and asked if he had everything and had picked up her corsage. "What corsage. I'm supposed to buy her flowers?" I told him not to worry about it and to just get ready. We arranged to meet at the restaurant to hand off the corsage we were going to pick up for him. When we arrived at the restaurant with the corsage, he informed us that he had not one, but two dates.

When we would go to listen to the school band in which he played the trumpet, we would always have trouble finding him because until his junior year he was the shortest boy in his class. The last two years he shot up like a bean on steroids and by the time he graduated, he was taller than me. The summer after graduation went with lightning speed and now he was on his way to college. My little boy was off to school and I knew our visits would be few until summer rolled around again.

We arrived at the campus, got him checked in, and went up to see his room. We came to the conclusion that he needed a loft bed and we set out to get the lumber to build it. As we put it together I was thinking that this was really it. My son was now a fine young man and was about to be on his own. The world can be an angry place and I was going to be too far away to help him if he ran out of gas or got a flat. I started to feel a little empty inside and a little helpless; I wasn't so sure that I wanted to leave him there. Then it occurred to me. I had done the same when I got out of high school and ran off to join the Air Force and leave for Texas. It was tough going at first, but the time away made me a better man for it.

As I pulled away, I saw my son waving in my rearview mirror. I pulled open the vanity mirror and took a look at myself and my wife was right. My eyes were moist and my lip was turned up. At that point, I knew it would be a long and lonely ride home. I had been around him as much as a non-custodial parent could be and I was there to help shape the story of his young life but I knew in the next chapter of his life I would have very little to do with the writing. I asked God to watch over him and protect him and then headed my car south. The miles seemed longer on the way home but each was filled with a different memory. I realized how blessed I was to have him for a son.

The Child Who Followed Me

As I walk the journey through my life
Since I have become a man
I know that I must place each step
As rightly as I can

For there is a child who follows me
He watches every step with care
And if I choose a lesser path
He just may follow there

The travel kit I like to use
My parents gave to me
Inside are tools like character
Truth and integrity

My granddad gave me something
To help me find the way
It's called a moral compass
And I use it every day

My uncles gave me ethics
To place there in my kit
My grandma said be who you are
Don't be a hypocrite

The tools my aunties handed down
They said came from above
So I followed in their footsteps
With unconditional love

They said when the path is darkest
That love will light the way
They said the more you use it
The brighter your next day

And when life throws you roadblocks
And struggles are everywhere
You can always hit your knees
And say a little prayer

So I took those tools to heart
And used them to shape his life
Whether I walked the path alone
Or together with my wife

And others in his family
Would sometimes lead the way
And help to shape him into
Who he's become today

Like the times spent with his grandpa
A man with a giant's heart
Work ethic, love, and character
He had down to an art

His mother's gift was independence
His grandma's, peace and love
And many pointed out the fact
There's guidance up above

His uncles taught him lessons
Each time he crossed their paths
To have a sense of humor
Don't be afraid to laugh

Stick up for the underdog
And if the cause is right
Don't back down to the bully
Stand your ground and fight

He took to heart each lesson
Throughout his childhood days
As if each mentor was a potter
And he a work of clay

Now as I look back down that traveled road
And see our footprints in the sand
I notice his are bigger now
My son's become a man

I can't take credit for his character
Or for his integrity
For they were merely gifts of love
Our loved ones shared with me

But as I stand and watch him take
His journey down life's path
I can see with every step he takes
His travel kit's intact

The Season of the Hunt

The sun was just touching the horizon when he reached the forest edge. He stopped and sparred a bit with a sapling, strengthening his neck muscles and practicing for what was soon to come. He stepped out in to the clover field and began to feed in an effort to build up body fat and weight for the months ahead.

The old farmer recognized him from the distance. He stood in the doorway of his old workshop and watched him for awhile. The old farmer had named him Pride the first time he saw him and his name fit him well. Over five years ago he had seen him and his twin brother, Glory, in the meadow. They were only a few days old and were with the old doe he called November. November's Pride and Glory. Pride was proud and he strutted about the meadow, and Glory bounded about like a jackrabbit without a care in the world. November met her fate this last summer as she tried to cross the busy highway. Glory last fall crossed the same busy stretch of highway and hurt his left rear leg. His antlers reflected that injury, the left side a perfect five long tines, but his right antler was palmated and smaller. Pride was in his prime and sported a perfect ten points this year, very wide and sweeping forward. A shooter the old farmer thought to himself as he watched Pride in the shadows that began to crawl across the clover plot.

Pride jerked his head up and stared off into the distance, looking for something, but not sure what he was searching for. He could sense it in the wind as it slithered through the cornfields and across the clover to his eager nostrils. Yet, he smelled nothing but the silence. Something was happening though; he could sense it. There was an urgency in the air and the wind seemed to bite a little more today than yesterday. This morning the ground was white with a light frost and a skim of ice was on the waterhole. Summer was long gone and fall was in full swing. The leaves were red and orange on the trees. The cornfields rattled in the gentle breeze, ears all turned down and ready for harvest. The apples were long gone from the wild trees and crabapples that a conscientious landowner had planted for his wildlife. All the acorns had been collected from the forest floor by hoarding fox squirrels trying to build a supply to sustain them through the winter months. Pride was fully aware that fall was here and winter was in the wings because his body was changing. He walked to an overhanging branch at the woodlot's edge and sniffed it, feeling obliged to leave his own scent upon it. Then he freshened the scrape beneath it and relieved himself in the fresh soil, leaving his track, a calling card for any doe that would have him and carry on his bloodline. There was the scent of a doe in that turned up earth and he knew he should pick up the trail and follow it to where she was waiting. If he did, he knew there could be dangers along the way because it was early in the rut and many other bucks would be searching her out, some ready to fight in order to win her over. There was a burning desire to hurry off in search of her, despite the danger of dominant bucks much larger than him and the injuries they could inflict. Yet something was different this evening and he felt a bit of unrest. It wasn't the two-legged creature called man that stood on the strange branch in the old oak tree; he was gone tonight and had been for several nights now. He had avoided him by staying downwind and out of bow range for a month now and had learned a valuable lesson as he watched his brother Glory wander close to the pile of corn that lay near the tree. When Glory had put his head down to eat, a stone-tipped stick came from the tree and took his life. He knew now that the two-legged creature meant danger and he should steer clear at all costs.

Again, he felt a burning inside to follow the sweet scent left in his scrape. He felt he was ready this year to take on most of his rivals; he was bigger and stronger than last year and he sported that heavy rack of ten points. But still something lingered in the still night air that he couldn't identify. There was something different, yet all to familiar this evening. He searched his memory back over the five and a half years he'd been alive and he began to remember the days when the snows came. The two-legged creatures carried fire sticks and they could reach out long distances with their stones. He saw his sister fall after that crack of thunder that came from one of those sticks. He was starting to remember now. It was the season of the hunt that was fast approaching. It was the eve before the opener and he knew now what tomorrow would bring. He would have to be alert and use his senses, stay upwind and stay hidden until darkness fell and he could move about freely. The burning had increased inside him and he knew he should go find her and spread his seed because tomorrow would bring uncertainties. It is survival of the fittest in the wild world and he was on his own now. It was up to him alone to pass on his genes and ensure his bloodline's survival. He walked back to the pawed up soil and picked up her scent. He inhaled deeply and began to feel a little different, his head was less clear and something pulled at him inside. He set out to find the one that would have him. The trail took him under the old oak tree with the funny branch and headed toward the standing corn. He put his nose to the ground and picked up the pace for she was waiting somewhere close, just beyond the fencerow where the little shack stood. Darkness fell as he reached the corn and he disappeared into it's rows. "Good night," the old farmer whispered, "Fare thee well."

A Diamond in the Gruff

The Warden, Colonel Clean-up, Old Grump, and Mr. Pick-up were all names we called him when he was out of earshot. When he was near we referred to him as Uncle Chuck, a big man with a gruff exterior who demanded a clean cook tent and a quiet camp after the lights went out. He rode herd on the new hunters in camp and we obeyed him as long as he was in sight. Having a DNR honcho in camp was kind of cool, but it did make us toe the line. I remember how he used to tell us he would call one of his officers if we didn't shape up. But we knew that when his DNR officer friends did come, they were way worse than we ever were. We would get to laughing at them because they would get to drinking and become quite funny. The more we would laugh, the madder Uncle Chuck would get.

He was always cleaning up after us. I remember searching through several inches of new fallen snow for Uncle Gale's teeth. It seemed that Captain Clean-up had pitched them out the night before because he thought it was a cup of water that one of us had failed to throw away. We got a lot of laughs out of that.

The Warden may have been tough and gruff but he was a sweetheart of a man too (but you didn't let him know you knew). I remember more than once, he would shove some change my way when my poker money got low or toss a roll of nickels on my lap so that I could keep on playing. And I remember every year that a check would come just before hunting season that would pay for our licenses. He wanted to make sure we would be able to hunt.

I remember laughing at him as we sat around the table after the opener talking about the deer we saw that day. Frank and Gale saw bucks, Jim shot one, and Gary saw several does. Tim shot a buck, Bill saw something brown and fast, and Basil saw a few in the birches. When it got to the Grump he always said something like "the blue jays seemed larger" or "the squirrels were bushier," but never do I remember him seeing any deer. I knew he

[87]

built a fire and smoked his pipe and read a book all in his blind. But not to see a single deer in all those years, he must have been blind. Well, I just learned he took pictures of deer he saw every year, including bucks too. I guess the joke was on us. He could have shot bucks, but he chose not to.

I remember another year when three of us new hunters caught some trout down at the spring where we got our drinking water. We had them in a bucket behind the tent and were looking at them when The Warden walked up on us. "What pray tell are you going to do with those fish? Are you aware that trout season is closed in November and you are breaking the law?" I replied with an explanation that we must have scooped them up by accident and were just going to let them go. "Good answer," he said, "Now get to it."

I remember dropping his name a time or two when we were out hunting and crossed paths with a DNR officer. One time in particular comes to mind. It was the first year there was a point system on ducks. It seemed that we were about three hundred points over our limit. The fact that we were just plain stupid and didn't know any better didn't seem to matter much, but the fact that we were Chuck Harris's nephews got us off the hook. Having a DNR honcho in the family was cool. We did learn a lot of respect for the outdoors from Uncle Chuck and we learned that the game laws were fair and we obeyed them. Uncle Chuck was a man who cared deeply about his family. He loved his job. He loved the time he spent with us at camp, and yes, he loved us. He loved his country. He believed that you should buy American, "especially cars." He thought a man should have a solid handshake. He was gentle in a rough sort of way. He was giving but didn't want the credit. He was our uncle and we were damn proud of it. He was a Marine I would want in my foxhole and a hunter I wish were still in camp. If I were to sum him up in a few short words, I would have to say he was a "Diamond in the Gruff."

I was proud to share camp with him.

A Sportsman's Prayer

In the meadows, swamps, and woodlots
I traipsed through when but a child
I learned to be a sportsman
And hunt the creatures of the wild

Men I revered taught me lessons
As I grew out of my youth
There is a sportsman's code of ethics
And your final judge is you

These men, they all wore Woolrich
They dressed in hunter's plaid
And I cherish every lesson
As I do each hunt we had

They said hunters have a purpose
But the chase, it must be fair
No creature deserves to suffer
So I heed this hunter's prayer

Lord if I choose to take a life
Guide my arrow straight and true
Or let me miss completely
The choice is up to you

If my arrow finds its mark
Let death be quick without the pain
And should I fail to feel this way
Don't let me hunt again

If I don't respect my quarry
Or my aim is less than good
I have no business hunting
I should not be in the woods

Break my fingers, take my eyes
Numb my feet, I shouldn't care
For if I'm not a sportsman
I have no business there

Never shoot more than what's needed
Never, ever waste the meat
Only hunt what is in season
Take no more than you can eat

These are rules I must live by
If sportsman is what I call myself
If these rules I can't abide by
I'll leave my weapons on the shelf

Lord, give me the wisdom
To hunt the way that's right
So I don't question my ethics
As I go to bed each night

Thank you Lord for giving me
The loving mentors that I had
These men who all wore Woolrich
And dressed in hunter's plaid

Deer Camp, My First Year

My bags were packed and my borrowed gun was stowed in the trunk in my older brother's car. It was November 13, 1972 and we were northbound for the opening of deer season in Michigan. We were headed to a tent camp in the northern lower half of the state where we would be spending a glorious week of deer hunting. The camp was backed up to a cedar swamp that was surrounded by thousands of acres of state, federal, and lumber company land. This was my first year of hunting deer and my first year at camp. I cannot begin to put into words how excited I was to finally join the men in a real hunting camp. My heart beat faster with every mile as we drove north, and I'm sure my brother got sick of me asking him how much farther?

As we turned off the blacktop and started down the first of several two-tracks that led back to camp, I could not sit still in my seat. When my brother finally said, "we're here," I thought my heart was going to jump out of my chest. There it was in all it's glory—the tent camp that I had only heard about in stories or seen in pictures because no one was ever allowed to walk on that hallowed ground until they possessed a hunting license at the age of fourteen. Awesome! Two old army tents stood among the pines with smoke coming out of the stovepipes. The ground was covered with a couple inches of snow and the air bit at my bare skin as I stepped out of the car. The tents seemed to call out to me, "Come let me warm you." I heeded their call and stumbled into one of them, almost falling into my uncle's bunk. Slow down young man. You have all week. Save some energy for the drag."

"The drag, what's the drag?" I asked.

"You know," he said, "when we bring deer out of the swamp."

"Oh yeah, I knew that," I said. Looking about the tent, I saw a three-burner cook stove, a large green cabinet with food in it, and a flat-topped wood burning stove they used to heat the tent. There was a huge pot of chili and a coffee pot setting on top, a table for eating and playing cards, and four cots. "Where do I put mine?" I asked.

"You set your cot up in the other tent with the rest of the young -guns" my uncle said. "Besides, it gets awfully loud in here at night and you'll get more sleep over there." I said thanks and was out the door into the next tent. This tent had a wood burning stove also and there was a teapot and large pan of water resting on top. There were already four cots set up, but we found room for ours and soon had our sleeping bags out and our clothes hung up on the wire that stretched across the top of the tent. There were also two lanterns hanging from the wire that would light the tents after the sun set.

Finally, I had made it! Deer camp with the grown-ups: three of my uncles on my mother's side and one of their good friends named Bill. There was my Uncle Gayle who I had hunted small game with before on his land down state. Uncle Gayle always had a smile on his face and seemed to enjoy life and everyone's company. Then there was my Uncle Frank who I had pheasant hunted with a couple times and also had two sons of his own there at camp. Uncle Frank always seemed to smile also, but I would soon learn that he was a prankster and brought to camp a bit of mystery, for a lack of better words. Then there was my Uncle Chuck who was an former Marine and DNR officer. He ruled the camp with an iron fist. Uncle Chuck, we learned early in life, demanded a lot of respect and we were more than happy to give it to him. All of these men had hearts of gold, but Uncle Chuck tried to disguise his with his sternness. Gayle and Chuck each had a son at camp also. These men had kept alive the spark that my father had instilled in us when it came to the out-of-doors and would further fan the flames as long as they were alive. We would always spend the holidays with them and would either be in the fields, woods, or sitting on a lake some-where depending on the season. A couple of weeks before squir-rel season, a check would show up in the mail that would pay for our hunting licenses for both small game and deer. Uncle Chuck wanted to make sure we were able to buy them and the check was always there. Bill was a friend of my uncles and he was a funny man who was always smiling, and along with my Uncle Frank helped to stir up a little bit of mischief about the camp. There was also a couple, Basil and Ragena, who stayed in a small trailer. They were older and had hunted with my uncle's parents when they first established the camp many years before. They continued the tradition every year. These were the giants who walked this hallowed ground we called deer camp. They were mentors and teachers and they were the epitome of true sportsmen.

I had no longer gotten my gear stowed away when someone yelled, "The chili is hot; come and get it." I think that was the best bowl of chili I had ever eaten, and would soon discover that everything tasted that way at deer camp. As soon as lunch was over, Uncle Gayle said we needed to get into the woods and get my blind set up so we don't have to go near it until opening morning. I grabbed a hatchet and we were off. I cannot put into words the excitement that was racing through my mind as we walked about the forest and found the perfect spot to build my blind. That excitement could only be rivaled by the feeling that would come on opening morning when someone yelled "Get up, it's almost daylight in the swamp." With my blind built, we headed back to camp and marked a trail so I could find my way to camp if I got cold on opening day. We cut some firewood and stacked it, and soon supper was on the table. After supper the dishes were washed and it was time to play cards. Penny poker was the game but the stakes often got as high as a nickel or dime for a really good hand. As we sat and played cards, many stories of hunts in the past were exchanged and I hung on every tale they told. One of my uncles said they had seen a huge bear as they drove into camp and they hoped that it wouldn't come back because it always went for the smallest person. I looked around and it didn't take long to notice that the smallest person was me. I slept with an axe that night and had my suitcase and a couple chairs stacked in front of the door so that I would hear anything that entered our tent. When my uncle came in to stoke our stove in the middle of the night, everybody was awakened by the sound of falling chairs and my uncle's cussing as he picked himself up off the ground yelling at me to put down the axe. The following day I got kidded quite a bit about almost clobbering one of my uncles, but I just laughed it off as an initiation into this group of hunters that I had for so long dreamed of being a part.

It was now the day before the opener. We cut and stacked more firewood and prepared our things for the next morning when we'd get to go after the elusive whitetail buck. We sighted in our rifles and for a borrowed gun, the thirty-two special that I had borrowed from my aunt seemed to fit me well and was dead on target. The day went by quickly and soon it was suppertime and then a quick card game again. As we were playing cards, my Uncle Gayle brought out a deer call that he said had helped him get a lot of bucks in the past. Unwrapping it from the packaged should have been a clue that he had never used it before, but I bit, hook, line, and sinker. He gave it to me and when I blew into it, it sounded like a cross between a sick duck and a crow. But, none-the-less, they said that's what a deer sounded like; I took it with anticipation of shooting the biggest buck in the woods. The smile on everyone's face should have tipped me off, but I was way too eager to learn any secret to success and heed any words of wisdom that would help me get my first buck. After all, these were seasoned veterans and they knew what they were talking about. I had for several years oohed in awe over the pictures of the heavy buck poles hanging next to these old army tents.

We played cards for a short while and then someone reminded us that we had a long day ahead of us tomorrow; five o'clock comes early, so we best hit the sack. Going to bed early was torture to me because I could not sleep. I was wide awake like when I was five on Christmas Eve; no chance I was going to catch much shut eye. As I lay in bed that night, I could hear each one of my uncles fall asleep because the minute they were out, the snoring began. The first one would start in and then the next and so on. Soon it was a chorus of unearthly noises that came from somewhere deep within. Strange noises I never would have guessed would come from a man's mouth, and other noises that I knew came from somewhere much lower and to the rear. So there I was trying to sleep with what sounded like chainsaws buzzing and foghorns tooting in the next tent. After about four hours of this, I was almost asleep when I heard the most frightening noise I had ever heard up to that point in my life. I quickly woke my brother who explained that it was just a bobcat and it wouldn't hurt me. The next thing I remember was being awakened by what sounded like a bunch of screaming banshees outside our tent. I yelled out to my brother to get his gun. His remark was less than pleasant and not filled with brotherly love. He told me to shut up and get to sleep and that I had better not wake him again or he would feed me to the pack of coyotes making all the racket. Some time after that, I finally drifted off and dreamt of coyotes tearing away at my flesh as my brother stood by watching and repeating, "I told you so."

"Daylight in the swamp" was the next thing I heard. I jumped out of bed and rushed outside thinking I had slept through the opener, only to find it was still very dark and that new fallen snow is cold on bare feet. I got dressed and went next door for a breakfast of pancakes and sausage and then quickly packed a lunch for the day. To say I was excited beyond anything I had ever experienced would be an understatement. I donned my long underwear and my sweatshirt and pants, a sweater and several pair of wool socks. Then I put on my snowmobile suit and my boots and was ready for the day. My uncles and my brother and several cousins had all put on red and black Woolrich hunting outfits and I remember wishing I could look like that someday. My brother was wearing the outfit that my father used to wear and I felt that he had to be the luckiest one of all and surely would have good luck in the woods. I gathered up everything and put it in my pack, grabbed my gun and shells, and we were on our way by flashlight beam to my blind. My uncle dropped me off and made sure I had my gun loaded; he made sure I was all set and then went on to his blind. By the time his flashlight beam disappeared, I was fit to be tied. A gun don't do much good if you can't see what you're shooting at, and here I was in the middle of the wild surrounded by bears, coyotes, bobcats, and Sasquatch. Coincidentally, my brother failed to mention until this morning that Sasquatch lived in this swamp, had eaten two hunters last year, and that I was the first to hunt in that part of the woods since it happened. So fear was in abundance that morning, at least in my small part of the forest as I sat there for the next half hour until the eastern sky began to lighten.

The darkness soon faded into shadows and with it went my fears. As the sun began to rise, I was filled with anticipation as I heard the first gun shot in the distant and then again, a closer one. I saw several deer that morning as they passed by on their way into the swamp, but try as I might, I could not put antlers on their heads. I watched several squirrels and numerous birds and even caught a glimpse of a beaver on the creek bank as the morning played out. Soon it was time for lunch and my uncle picked me up and we went back to camp for barbeques. Then we headed back out to our blinds until dark. That night, as we sat around the table, we all talked about the deer we saw and my uncles and brother decided they would go deep into the cedar swamp the next day but that I should return to my blind on the outside of the swamp.

The second day was much like the first except that I would be hunting the edge by myself and I went to my blind on my own. Fear was again in abundance as I made my way to my blind except this time I had loaded my gun before I left camp and the wait for daylight was not as long because I stayed at camp as long as I could. When I got to my blind, I started to unpack my bag and lit a can of sterno to keep my hands warm. While digging through my bag, I found the temporarily forgotten deer call my uncle had given me. As the sun began to rise I started blowing on the call expecting the deer to come running; I continued to blow it all morning. I saw no deer and very few squirrels and birds, but I did hear a lot of shooting coming from the swamp. So, I thought it would just be a matter of time before one came running to my call. I returned to camp for lunch that day and my brother was back at camp already, along with my Uncle Chuck and a couple cousins. My brother was very excited because he had shot not just one, but two bucks that morning, and I needed to come help him drag them out. He also said my uncle Gayle had shot one and we had our work cut out for us. Having our work cut out for us was an understatement; the swamp was wet and tangled and as my uncle put it "a hellhole to get a deer out of."

Nonetheless, I was pumped up and gladly went along for the drag. What was a half-hour walk into the swamp as we negotiated the blow-downs and standing water turned out to be a three-hour drag out. We were soaked up to our waist with swamp water and everything above that was soaked in sweat. My uncle would walk ahead of us with all the guns and then we would follow behind with the deer. Every other step it seemed we would sink down to our thighs in the muck and more than a dozen times I heard "Damn Beavers" come out of someone's mouth. When we got to the creek I saw the damage that the beavers had done and understood where those earlier comments came from. The water was backed up and a lodge stood in the middle of the pond; much of the swamp was under water because of the dam the beavers had built.

We rinsed the deer out in the icy waters, finished the drag to the trucks, and took them to camp to hang on the buck pole. We were cutting off a hindquarter to cut up for supper when my Uncle Chuck reminded us those deer needed tags on them. We were only allowed to shoot one buck a year back then so I was elected to tag the other deer. My Uncle Chuck was leaving to go home that night but he refused to tag it and so it was my responsibility.

What angered me to no end would eventually turn into a life lesson for me and would further strengthen the respect I had for that man who taught me a lesson of responsibility. My first deer season and I had to tag someone else's buck; I was a little mad to say the least and I let my brother know it. I did get to return to the woods the following morning before we broke camp and one of my uncles said they would tag it if I shot one. But that was not to be. We broke camp and headed home with both bucks atop our car.

I played the part well of the successful hunter as hundreds of cars passed us and gave us the thumbs up. After all, they didn't know they were both my brothers and I wasn't about to tell them. Deer camp 1972 was over and I was already anticipating next year's hunt and I was sure I was going to shoot my brother's deer. On the way home he thanked me for his deer. He said if I hadn't been making all of that racket with that dang deer call that I never would have scared those deer to him and Uncle Gayle. Once again, hook line and sinker; but hey, I got to walk among giants on that hallowed ground and hunt with my heroes. And next year there would be two more hunters in camp, both younger than me. I had a whole year to plan their initiation. Awesome!

Gammy Creek

I listened to my uncle's tales
When I was a wild-eyed child
They talked about the hunts they shared
And the creatures of the wild
And while looking at their photos
Of them dressed in hunter's plaid
They recounted every moment spent
With sportsman friends they had
They talked about a hunting camp
and a place called Gammy Creek
Where the deer run wild, the bear roam free
And the best of hunters meet
Where friends are there, the hunt is fair
And memories are made
And strangers soon are lifelong pals
Whose friendships never fade
Where your trials and tribulations
and the stresses of the day
As you take gun or bow in hand
All seem to fade away
When your game bag comes home empty
or the buck pole doesn't sag
They said it didn't matter much
It's about the time you had
They'd speak about the hunts they shared
And their eyes would twinkle bright
And they said it just got better
With the fading of the light
When coyotes bayed at the setting sun
in a chorus with a loon
And a horned owl screeched its welcome
To a rising hunter's moon
When the game of chase was over
and the day came to an end
This was the time they cherished most
as they gathered with their friends

Well, my uncles have since left us
For the happy hunting ground
And several seasons passed before
This revelation that I found
I'd searched their maps and charts in vain
To find this Gammy Creek
Where the deer run wild, the bear roam free
And the best of hunters meet
Then it came one day while hunting
These voices upon the wind
They sounded just like my uncles
They said I needed to look within
Search inside your heart and soul boy
And we're sure that you will find
It's more than just a place to go
Gammy Creek's a state of mind
So surround yourself with buddies
And family if you can
For the bounties of the wild are ours
As stewards of the land
And when the coyote bays at the setting sun
In a chorus with the loon
And the horned owl screeches welcome
To a rising hunter's moon
When the game of chase is over
And the day comes to an end
This is the time to cherish most
With your family and your friends
Then talk about the hunt you had
And the one that got away
Swap your tales and truths and lies
And plan for other days
When your game bag comes home empty
Or the buck pole doesn't sag
Remember it doesn't matter
It's about the time you had

Game Bag Empty, Memory Full

I learned at a very young age that you don't always fill your game-bag or come home with a stringer full of fish every time you take to the woods or soak a line. If you did, then we would call it killing and catching instead of hunting and fishing. I can't begin to count how many times I have returned from one of those trips empty handed, yet still had an awesome time afield. It never fails that after one of those jaunts someone will ask me how my trip was and have a puzzled look on there face when I say fantastic. "But you didn't get a deer or you didn't catch any fish. How can that be so fantastic?" It's at this point that I think to myself, what a shame. They haven't got a clue as to what it's all about. They don't understand why I go to the woods or why I go to the river, and for them I feel a bit of sorrow, for they are missing out.

There are some who do hunt and fish and measure their time afield or at water's edge by what goes into their freezer. If all they are after is a meal, then I hope they are satisfied. If it's just bragging rights they're after then I wish them little luck. I have hunted and fished with a few people like that, but only a couple times because they don't understand either. For me, it's all about the time spent in the woods or on the stream that wets my whistle.

I believe what a hunter stalks or a fisherman casts for is not as important as just being out there in the company of friends and family. The camaraderie is captivating when you share nature at its finest with someone who truly understands that it's the experience that counts. I admit that as a young hunter, there was an urgency in me to fill my tag. As a young angler, I wanted so much to come home with a fat Steelie. I realized later in life that I was just seeking bragging rights and although I was successful, it often left me feeling hollow when someone else came home empty handed. Don't get me wrong, I love venison. And a fresh venison steak on the grill with a little Lawry's seasoning salt is hard to beat; even prime rib pales in comparison. But the meat is just a bonus and will never go to waste.

Many times, I've stood waist deep in ice cold water leaning heavy into a current that would like to take me downstream and out to Lake Michigan. As you cast your line in the pre-dawn darkness you often have to stop and remove the ice from your rod-eyes so you can cast on. Nothing, not even a strike. You know the water is a little too cold and the Steelies are backed up in some hole down stream, but you keep casting. Your fingers and toes begin to numb from the bitter cold and you know the fish aren't biting. You may start to question your presence. You look around to see who is still with you just as the sun starts to turn the sky crimson and the first of the morning light has arrived. You see steam rising from the black water and there upstream, you see the silhouette of a brother or a buddy and again you realize why you're here. Because you can be, that's why. And now for the time being, all is right in your world. You make your way against the current, back to the bank and grab your thermos to pour yourself a steaming cup. With any luck your fingers will steal some of the warmth. You sit down on the bank and watch as your buddy casts on. You watch a mink across the river make its way up and down the bank in search of his breakfast. You pour another cup and wade out to your partner and hand it to him. You ask if he's seen the mink on the other shore. He has, and he hands you his rod to take a few casts as he takes the cup of coffee and thanks you. "Beautiful morning," he says, "Sure beats work." You nod in agreement and silently thank your Creator for this day.

Or maybe you have darkness on your side and you use it to conceal your approach to your stand and silently climb into it. You sit motionless in the predawn darkness and watch your breath float upwards like a ghost rising from a tomb. You feel the cold pushing in around you, searching for a place to enter your layers of clothing and nip at your skin. Your eyes squint, scanning the darkness for movement. Your ears work equally hard listening for crunched leaves or sticks being broken under the heavy hooves of a nocturnal buck returning from his rendezvous, now on his way to his hiding place for the day. As the horizon begins to redden and the last of the stars are plucked from the morning sky, a lone ringneck rooster cackles. Then, it's like someone flicked a switch and the woods begins to come alive. A crow caws and instantly a shock gobble comes from a distant tom turkey. Then a red squirrel chatters out a good morning and a blue jay answers. The music of the forest creatures provides a soothing soundtrack that helps to chase away your troubles. There is something to be said from a mental health point-of-view that this is where I belong. This is the medicine I need to protect my sanity, and for a time, I am at peace.

These are pleasures I need in my life, and are better than any drug a doctor can prescribe. These pleasures make me feel alive and in control of my small part of the world. No one forces me to come here. It's on my own accord, and it's a freedom that breathes life into this tired body. I choose who I want to spend the time with, not some boss back in the workplace. I have many friends in my life, but there are only a few I choose to hunt and fish with. Only those few share the same sportsman's ethics that I do. They have the same love and respect for the creatures we seek and they understand that when dispensing death is the task at hand dignity must be maintained or the death becomes meaningless. A wild life cut short by a razor tipped arrow or a well-placed bullet is no laughing matter. It's serious and not to be taken lightly. A spawning female Steelie is not to be horsed in and then when landed, should be handled carefully if you plan on releasing her. She holds within her the beginning of many a generation of her kind. These friends have proven to me that they feel the way I do and have earned the right to share a camp with me. I know they feel the same way about me or I wouldn't be invited into theirs. They get as much joy in me taking an animal as they would it they had shot it themselves. They would gladly give up a better stand if they thought I might get a shot, and I would do the same for them. They are there to pick up a blood trail and won't give up until we find the animal and it is on the buck pole. If for some unfortunate reason we don't find an animal, they know why I feel the way I do, with the sick feeling in my stomach and the heavy heart. They understand why I question my competence as an archer even when they know how much I practice; they have been there and felt the same way.

They feel the same way I do when I turn a spawning female loose. I hold it in the current until it can swim away on it's own. For the lack of better words, it's a feeling of responsibility not unlike relaxing your bow and letting a smaller buck walk away. Death can be at your fingertips and you chose not to break out the stringer or release the bow string, because you truly believe that your actions at that very moment determine whether or not in the future you may come across some of their offspring and a smile forms somewhere inside you and forces it's way outward, gracing your face. You are a steward of the land and it's creatures, and again, you have done a small part to help insure their future.

For a time you walked with blood brothers in the lap of God and though you came home with nothing for the freezer you came away with memories you will forever cherish. And truth be told, I'll take the latter. When the last of the game or fish makes it's way from the freezer to the table and are removed by anxious hands and shoveled into hungry mouths, then the wait is on until next season. Not so with my memory banks as they are always overflowing, I can make a withdrawal at a second's notice and I'm always ready to share a story. God has blessed me with special friends and relatives who share my brand of sportsman's ethics and respect the game as I do. For that, I am forever grateful; I am blessed and highly favored.

The Double Lunger Club

October was taking an eternity getting here, or at least it seemed that way to the young hunter. This would be his first season in the woods that he was old enough to carry a bow and arrow. He had practiced religiously and was shooting good groups that even a seasoned veteran would be happy with. The regular bow season was still two weeks away when his Dad told him that he was able to go on the youth hunt in September if he behaved the rest of the week. With four siblings, and trouble makers on the bus and at school, it would be a challenge. But he was up for the test and on Friday his dad said, "Get your stuff around."

The next morning was long in coming and excitement was in the air as he dressed for the hunt. They arrived at the woods and climbed into the shack. The hunt was on. Anticipation and excitement filled the shack and it was all he could do to hold still. He was twelve-years-old and this would be his first hunt. He just knew he was going to get a monster. He sat there with his dad for what seemed like forever when they saw a couple deer approaching. It looked like two doe and to the first-time hunter, they looked huge. His father had told him he could take a doe if the opportunity presented itself and so he started preparing for the shot. The larger of the two gave him a broadside shot and with Dad's blessing he drew and released. The arrow sped to its target. His aim was perfect and his arrow found its mark. A double lung shot and the animal would not go far before it expired.

His hands started shaking, his knees started knocking, and as they walked up on the animal, he could hardly contain his emotions. As he looked down at those deep brown eyes he felt a bit uneasy and a bit saddened as he realized how death is so final in the natural world. He felt a bit guilty for taking such a beautiful animal's life and had a tear in his eye when his Dad slapped him on the back and said, "Awesome shot, Son. Way to go. I'm proud of you." He snapped back to cool city and had a smile as big as a barn on his camoed face.

"You got yourself a young buck, Son. See these buttons on his head? Well, let's get this thing gutted," his dad said as he took out a knife. He cut into the young buck's stomach and that feeling of uncertainty was back. The insides were not as cool as the outside, and they stunk too, but with Dad's help it was soon over and they were dragging it to the truck. They loaded it up and were on their way to the buck pole in their hometown. A pair of peacocks couldn't have strutted any more proud than these two as they unloaded their trophy and drug it towards the pole. When it was up, they realized it was small compared to the other animals hanging there. His dad reminded him that those were all taken with a gun and that he should be proud of his because he had done it with archery equipment. He was the youngest hunter there and the only one with a bow kill; he got an award for that. He was even more proud when he got home and was able to show it off to the rest of the family. Dad was just as excited and with good reason. He made a few phone calls to some buddies to brag about his son. His brothers teased him a little about the size of his trophy and the next day at school, they teased him even more. He was feeling a little hurt and a little less proud because of the influence his peers had on him by the time he got home. As he was telling his dad about his day and the tongue-lashing he had taken from the boys at school, his dad said, "They're just jealous. Don't let it bother you." He then pulled from his pocket a letter and handed it to his son. The young hunter tore it open and as he read the following words, a smile returned to his face. His chest stuck out a little further and he seemed to grow a couple inches taller. Congratulations, Son.

Your dad let us see the pictures of you and your buck and shared with us your hunt. That was an awesome shot you made on it. You must have done everything right to be able to get that close and make the perfect shot. A double lung shot is the best shot, the perfect shot, and the only shot a bow hunter should aim for. You pulled it off. You should be proud of yourself because you waited and didn't rush your shot. A lot of hunters would have flung an arrow as soon as they saw those deer, and a less than desirable shot could mean a lot of suffering for the animal.

You took the time to do it right.

You now are a member of the Double Lunger Club. The Double Lunger Club (DLC) is an unofficial club of conscientious bow hunters who hold off for the perfect shot. Sometimes this means coming home without anything except the feeling that you made the right choice. Members of the DLC have found that an empty buck pole is always better than a wounded animal suffering because of a shot taken in greed. We have learned to pass up shots even at trophy bucks if the double lung shot does not present itself. A membership in the DLC does not come with any special prize, or money, or even fame. It does, however, come with piece of mind that when you lay your head down on your pillow at night, you have a clean conscience knowing you did everything you could to keep that animal from suffering. You will know the comfort of a good night's sleep where you don't question your ethics. You win the admiration of your fellow members and will be welcome at their campfires and hunting camps. Your name is passed along to other members of this club and you are held in high regards as a hunter who has earned the honor of this elite fellowship. You earn the right to call yourself a true sportsman.

When you took that deer, you accomplished something that was very hard to do. Many archers and even gun-hunters don't get a deer for several years after they start hunting. You took a buck with a bow and arrow, and that is no small feat. The fact that there were bigger deer on the buck pole should not matter because you took yours with an arrow and those others were taken with a gun. It takes a lot more skill and patience to take one your way. Most people can't even hit a target with an arrow and you pulled off an awesome shot. Don't let anyone tell you anything different. Don't let them steal your victory. You deserve it and we at the DLC. know what kind of hunter you really are— the kind we want to be in the woods with.

Your dad was very proud and it is awesome that he got to share the hunt with you. Cherish that and always remember the way you felt both leading up to the shot and when you walked up on your trophy laying there. If you were nervous and your hands and legs were shaking, that's normal. I hope you never lose that sensation. If you felt pride in yourself for the shot you took, that's great; you should. If you felt saddened by seeing it lying there dead, that too is a part of the hunt and is nothing to be ashamed of. All three of these feelings should be present every time you kill a deer if you did everything right. I rushed a shot once and got a bad hit on the animal. The track job took six hours and the animal was still alive. I had to put another arrow in it and it expired. Sure, I finally got it, but that animal suffered all that time. It was a real nice buck and when the guys back at camp wanted to celebrate, I didn't feel like it. The sweetness of the victory was soured by the bad placement of that shot and the weight of regret far outweighed any pleasure I got from taking that animal. It lays heavy on my conscience. I have since passed up many, many bucks waiting for that perfect shot and I got more pleasure knowing that a lesser man would have taken that shot but I chose to wait.

They say when an animal is hit in both lungs that they rarely live more than 11 seconds. Although they can run a long way in that time, they feel very little pain. That, in our book, is the only shot to take, and you did just that. Awesome job. We are all proud of you and welcome you to the Double Lunger Club. May your arrows fly true, may your track be short, and may you never have to question your ethics. Fellow hunters of the DLC.

With the letter came a certificate of membership into the DLC. That night, as he sat down to dinner, the venison tasted a little sweeter, the teasing bit a little less, and he slept with the satisfaction that despite what the others said, he did it right. He fell asleep with visions of bigger bucks, shorter tracks, hunts shared with his dad, and those other hunters who truly understand what hunting is all about. He slept sound knowing the ethics his father had instilled in him were intact and that even though it wasn't the biggest buck on the pole, there were those that were proud of him despite of that. He took the only perfect shot, pulled it off without a flaw, and earned his way into the DLC.

Why I Hunt

You ask me why I hunt. It's hard to explain if you haven't been there. It's a feeling of freedom, a sense of belonging, and an escape. It's not so much a thing I do, but a place I go. A place where all the burdens of everyday life are lifted from my chest, a place where the modern world and all of its pressures are removed and linger somewhere beyond the woodlot or swamp in which I am hunting.

As you climb into your tree-stand in the predawn darkness and lean back against the tree that is your hiding spot for next few hours, a feeling of peace comes over you. And as the woods settle around you, you are absorbed into your surroundings. As you sit in the darkness, the silence is deafening and pushes in all around you. The last stars of the night begin to disappear and the eastern sky begins to show color. The magic hour has arrived as the night slowly gives way to the day. The woods begin to come alive. Slowly at first, as the last owl says goodnight and the first song of a nearby bird seems to say "Welcome to our sanctuary." At first you feel awkward, all most guilty. It's such a gentle place and you've come to take an animal's life. You begin to question your presence, and your right for that matter, to even be in such a beautiful place. But you have been there before and it's always the same. You know the value of a predator; without them there would be no wildlife. Death is a part of nature, a way to control the numbers so they don't overpopulate and destroy their habitat. You know that if the opportunity presents itself, you may take a life today, and you feel that you're ready. Its always an emotional time though. You feel a sense of loss each time you take an animal, for you have great respect for the creature you are seeking. If you don't feel that loss, then you have no business in the woods, for you are not a hunter but a thief. You must respect the creature you seek and you must wish it no pain and suffering. You must do your part to see that death comes quick and clean, for life is a precious, a serious thing not to be taken lightly.

As the darkness turns to dawn and the shadows begin to fade, your world begins to come alive with activity. You sit there quietly and take in nature's beauty as the morning plays out. Squirrels begin to rustle in their nests and are soon moving out on to the branches to catch the first warming rays of the morning sun as it touches the highest of the treetops. A distant crow rants and raves about something as a tom turkey gobbles, as if to scold it for breaking the silence. A ruffed grouse steps up on a fallen log and begins to move his wings, slowly at first, but then, like a drummer warming up, he picks up the pace until only a blur of his wings can be seen. And then, as quickly as he began, it's over and he steps back off the log.

A red squirrel chatters a good morning and a woodpecker picks up the beat where the ruffed grouse left off. A blue jay lands on a limb and screams out a warning as a red fox comes trotting into view, back and forth across the woodlot, searching for a morning meal. The woods are again silent, as each creature freezes in its tracks, not wanting to be the fox's breakfast.

Another predator shares your world, unaware of your presence. For if he knew you were there, he would be gone in a blink. You marvel at his beauty and whisper a thank you to the Creator for sharing him with you. And then, as quickly as he came, he's gone and you hear that same jay in the distance as he again reveals the fox's presence in another part of the forest.

You tell yourself to sit still so that you are not discovered. You tug your gloves down over your wrists and pull up your zippers as far as they go, wishing they would reach just a little farther so there would be no opening around your neck. The cold is trying its best to get inside your layers of clothing and chase away the warmth that allows you to stay still and comfortable. It wants to drive you away from this place. The forest again, begins to come alive with the sounds of birds and squirrels. A red squirrel runs down a beech tree and out on that same log the grouse was drumming on a few minutes earlier. There, he chatters out as if to say, "You missed us old fox. Good riddance."

And then, a blur of brown, and white, and red, and he's silent as he's lifted in the talons of a red tailed hawk toward the rising sun. Death came swift, clean and painless as death should. Another predator in the woods, who like the fox, needs meat to survive. Meat cannot be meat without death being present. It's been that way since the beginning.

The sun has now broken the horizon and the trees and forest floor have come alive with color. What a beautiful place the woods of autumn are. So many reds and yellows splashed about. As I take in the colors, I hear it. It's the sound of crunching leaves, the unmistakable rustle of footsteps. I freeze, motionless, and strain to hear it again. Where is it? What is it? How close has it gotten? Is it down wind? Have I been busted? My heart is beating out of my chest and I swear it's going to hear me. There it is again. It's closer now and I turn, ever so slowly, to see the source. It's a yearling doe coming down a trail to my right and behind her, a larger doe. They are in no hurry. They are feeding on acorns and red maple leaves as they make their way toward me. The yearling seems only concerned with what's to eat on the ground. The older doe is more concerned about her back-trail; she turns several times and looks behind her. She lifts her head up and tests the air for any dangers that may be up-wind.

I smile to myself. This time I hung my stand in the right place and my presence is not detected. The older doe still seems uneasy and I check her back-trail again just as she does. Then, I see the object of her concern, the same thing I am here for—a buck. He looks to be a fork-horn, a healthy deer. His neck is beginning to swell and his antlers are shiny, all polished from rubbing them on saplings as he readies himself for the upcoming rut. As he approaches, I can see brow-tines. He's a six-point, a fine deer. He would make great table fare.

My breath is coming harder now. My heart is racing as I ready myself. My right leg begins to shake and my knees feel like they may give out. I try my hardest to be silent as I bring my bow around and ready myself for a shot. As his head goes behind a tree, I try to draw my bow. It feels as if it's set at ninety pounds, and I struggle to pull it back. Then I freeze as the buck jerks his head up and looks in my direction. A few seconds seem like hours before he relaxes. I strain against the pull of the bow as I wait for him to move into my shooting lane. Finally, he's there and I take aim. I line up my sight pin with that sweet spot just behind his shoulder blade. I hold it for a few seconds and then relax my bow. I say to myself, *Grow large young fellow and go spread your seed. Always stay downwind and stay out of the road.*

Today was not the time. If so, then my hunts would be over for the year and I'm not ready to give this up. I sit through the daylight hours and take in God's beauty, watching several more deer; but I never again lift my bow. I had a buck and doe tag in my pocket and any one of those deer would have been legal had I wanted to take one. Killing a deer is only a small part of the hunt; being out there is what matters. There will be other days, and other hunts. If I'm lucky, maybe then; maybe not.

You ask me why I hunt. Because I can, that's why. I am fortunate to live in a country that allows me this privilege. God has blessed me well.

Also, because I feel a need to take responsibility, for at least a part of the meat that I eat. I know that meat does not just materialize in some supermarket freezer somewhere, but that a creature had to lose its life to be there on our tables.

I hunt because when I am in the woods, I feel the presence of many of my loved ones that I have lost, those who also enjoyed the hunt and shared this love with me. I replay their memories in my mind as I sit and listen to the sounds of this wondrous world. And sometimes I hear their voices whispers in the gentle breeze that brings colorful leaves floating to the ground through the treetops. This is the place I feel the closest to them.

The sunset is beautiful, splashes of amber melt into shades of red, and then purples, as the sun drops below the horizon. And then darkness rushes in and begins to chase away what remains of an autumn day.

I climbed down from my stand in the encroaching darkness and as I reached the ground, I felt a bit of unrest. I stood there for several moments taking in the scents and sounds of the night. A gentle breeze began to blow and it rattled the leaves in the trees like Ezekiel's bones. A coyote yips in the distance and then all is silent. I could smell the tarsal gland of the buck that was here earlier and the strong scents coming from the scrape he freshened as he passed through. I felt safe in this refuge and for the moment, all was right in the world. I was hesitant to leave this haven, for I knew what was out there. Hiding, lurking somewhere beyond the woodlot, out past the cornfield, somewhere between the clover and my home, it lay in ambush like the puma. I walked silently, ever so careful to place my feet where there were no sticks that would call attention to my departure. My pace quickened as I left the edge of the corn.

As I neared my home, I felt its presence, small at first and then overwhelming. The everyday stresses and strains of a civilized world had found me, and like a plague in some horror flick, tried its best to enter my head. It took up its never-ending dual with my sanity, waging war against my piece of mind, fatiguing my flesh and bones with its heavy burden, and trying its damnedest to wipe the smile from my face. But I am a bow hunter, and I have hope. For October is my salvation. It is the season of rejuvenation for a hunter's soul. It is fuel in his or her gas tank and carries them through the year. This is only the first of October; there is always tomorrow, and the next day, and the next day and the next . . . Well, you get the picture.

If you are a bow hunter, you know the place I go and the place I come back to. For a moment, in this dash that we call life, I sat in a lofty perch like an eagle. Waited in ambush like a cougar, and moved silently across the forest floor like a native of this land. For a short time, I was a part of a grander scheme and was accepted as a predator in a wilder, yet gentler piece of this world we live.

This woodlot is a refuge where I can run away for a short time from my stresses and pressures of this modern life that was forced upon us by a changing and unforgiving world. Although I did not take a buck today my hunt was successful because for a moment I escaped, and walked with spirits that have passed before, took in a deep breath of October and for a millisecond felt whole again. As I went to bed that night I thanked the Lord for the day behind me, asked for many more to come and then drifted off to sleep with pleasant dreams of long tines, wide racks and heavy footprints in new frost.

Death, Don't Let It Become Meaningless

The first time I was at the business end of a shotgun with a mission to get a kill under my belt, I was at a much different place in my life. I was twelve-years-old, toting a new shotgun I had bought with money earned from mowing lawns and baling hay. At my side was my guide for the day, a mentor of mine and someone I both admired and loved dearly, my grandfather. He had me out on a rabbit hunt and I was more than eager to shoot my first. That opportunity came about twenty minutes into the hunt when we spotted a rabbit hiding next to a log. It must have thought it was invisible to us because it sat there and never moved as we approached to within only a few feet.

"Take the end of its nose off." I remember my grandfather saying. I took careful aim down the barrel and lined the bead up with its nose. I squeezed the trigger and all hell broke lose. The rabbit flipped over four feet into the air and when it landed, it let out the most awful cry I had ever heard in my life. It kept squealing and my grandfather said to shoot it again.

"No," I said, "I'm ready to go home." He walked over to the rabbit that laid there kicking and making that God-awful sound. He picked it up and twisted its head clean off.

"If you are going to start something then you need to finish it," He said. "We still need one more to make a meal." So we continued the hunt and soon had another one in the game bag. The second one he shot, and after the sound of the twenty-two rifle, that rabbit never moved again. "That's how we are supposed to do it," he said.

When we got home, we cleaned those rabbits and although it didn't set to well with my stomach, we soon had them ready for Grandma to fry up. I remember my grandmother saying we did a good job of killing those rabbits because she didn't find any shot pellets in them. Grandpa told her it was because we were good hunters and we knew what we were doing. He looked at me and winked, and we kept the rest of the hunt to ourselves. I remember how good those rabbits tasted and how proud I was to be putting meat on the table. If I had been on that hunt by myself, and if it unfolded the same way, I don't know if I ever would have shot another rabbit. I think my grandfather knew that, and that was why we stayed out there and took another.

Until that moment, I never really thought about the animal I was hunting being in pain, or not dying quickly or quietly. I guess I just thought that you pull the trigger and you have meat. It doesn't work that way though, and that is what makes hunting so personal. Because death is so final, one must be prepared to except that and do everything in his power to make sure it comes quickly and as painlessly as possible. A good hunter or true sportsman has more than likely passed up many more shots than he has taken because they were not perfect. Many a sportsman have seen bigger bucks than any that he has taken, but he let them walk instead of trying a less than perfect shot at them.

I work with a guy who claims to be a good hunter, and he does have a few bucks to his credit. One day during shotgun season, I walked up on a conversation he was having with a couple of his hunting partners. They were laughing and having a good time and I thought I might hear a good joke if I stopped and listened. What I heard was something that made me so mad I almost punched him right there and then. It seemed that the day before two of them were out hunting and one had shot a button buck. It was running straight away from him when he shot. It went down rather quickly but when they walked up to it, it was bleating. Its rear end was paralyzed and it was trying to get up. They stood there and laughed at it and watched it for several minutes before it finally expired. Why this seemed to bring joy and laughter to these individuals, I have not a clue. I expressed my concerns about idiots of that caliber being allowed to own a gun. I went on to inform them that any permission I had granted them to hunt on my land had at that moment been withdrawn. I let them know they were the epitome of how every animal rights activist viewed hunters. I let them know I wanted to stomp them into a mud puddle and walk them dry because so called hunters like them are what gives sportsmen like the rest of us a bad name. They could not understand why I was getting so upset. I was upset! And it takes a lot to ruffle my feathers. I apologized for walking up on their conversation only because I thought maybe they would apologize for their shortcomings and inadequacies when it came to hunting. It didn't happen though, and I guess I wasn't so surprised. For a split second, I could see why any anti-hunter could harbor so much hate for hunting.

These guys are still friends of mine because we work in the same place, but I will not extend a welcome to my property and I refuse to share a hunt camp with them. My time spent afield and in my hunt camps is reserved for those that better understand the taking of life and how vital it is to do it quickly and humanely. When your goal is to take a life, dignity must be maintained or that death becomes meaningless. If you don't respect the animal you are after, then you ought not be there.

As a modern day society, we tend to isolate ourselves from death. We live miles away from the slaughterhouses and have no idea how our meat is processed and for that matter, don't care to know. We don't want to consider how an animal died and actually became the meat which satisfies our hunger. The closest we dare get to taking responsibility for the meat we consume is to look at the ads in the newspaper and make sure we get the best price at the supermarket. If we let someone else handle the funeral arrangements, then we don't have to think about it or get our hands dirty.

For me, it's important that I take some responsibility for what I eat, so I don't take for granted that my meal was once a living creature that God gave us dominion over. If I take part in its death, then to me its life was not meaningless, and each time I feel a sense of satisfaction that I did everything right. If I didn't do it correctly and its death was not quick and clean, then I feel no satisfaction. The meat is harder to swallow and I beat myself up mentally each time I reach into the freezer. Its pain weighs heavy on my conscience and I question my ability as a hunter. This is how it should be if you choose to hunt, and I know the ones I call my hunting companions feel the same way I do.

I am blessed to have many relatives and good friends who believe in and practice the same ethics I do, and I thank God for them. It is with this caliber of hunters that I am drawn to and enjoy being with in the fields and forests, for they understand the true meaning of a sportsman. They understand that having a game bag sagging on your back, or a fine buck hanging on the pole, is always a bonus. The fact that you are able to be afield with good friends is what the hunt is all about. If you are a hunter, and the most important part of your hunt is having bragging rights, then you have a long way to go. I hope you get there. Drawing your bow and putting that pin on that sweet spot behind a buck's shoulder is an awesome feeling, but nothing compared to relaxing your string and knowing that he could have been yours, but you opted to wait for something larger. When you can reach the end of the season with an empty tag and still consider it a successful year, you are that much closer to understanding what it is really all about.

I am a steward of the land that I own and I do all I can to make it wildlife friendly. I truly respect the animals I hunt and have let many, many more animals walk than I have taken. If the perfect shot does not present itself, then I will not shoot. When a buck comes into range, yet doesn't offer that perfect shot, it is at that moment when character shows through, when there is no one around to answer to except oneself. Do you take the shot? If you chance a less than perfect shot, then you have no respect for that animal and are no better than the poacher that takes one out of season or after dark. Your character is flawed and you might introduce that animal to undo pain and suffering because of your greed. Even when the perfect shot presents itself, circumstances out of your control may be present, and again, your character shows through. There will be a blood trail to follow and it may be hard to figure out; many a hunter have given up way too early. The track job should never end until the animal is found or every possibility has been considered before giving up the trail. I don't know how many times hunters have told me they gave up the track because it was late and they couldn't find any more signs. Yet they returned the next morning and found the animal only a few yards ahead of where they left off. Others talk of returning in the morning to make larger circles around the last sign, at which point they pick up the trail and find the animal.

I believe that when we pick up a bow or gun with the intent to take a life, we have an obligation to do it as humanely as possible. And once a shot is taken, we should not give up the track until every possibility has been exhausted. Anything less would be a disrespect to the animal and is simply not acceptable.

That first hunt of mine was over three decades ago and I still recall it like it was yesterday. The rabbit may have died that day, but the sound it made stayed behind, forever etched in my memory bank to remind me that if I'm going to take a life, I have to do it right. Do it as quickly and as painlessly as possible, or don't even draw a bead, line up a sight pin, or center a crosshair; you don't have that right. Hunting is not so much a right as it is a privilege. We have a responsibility to do it correctly or not to do it at all.

Man as a Predator

Does man have the right to hunt?

I believe man has the responsibility to keep the number of animals in check. If you asked me that same question one hundred years ago, I may have had a different answer. I doubt it though, because I love to hunt and I love the taste of venison. One hundred years ago was a different time though. There was much more countryside, much more wilderness, millions of acres more of forest, and many, many more predators. Wolf, bear, cougar and coyote all roamed the country and preyed upon the wildlife. They kept the herds in check by culling the weak and sick and the old and injured, and in doing so, they kept the populations where they should be, where the land could handle them. Since then, man has encroached upon the land and now, most of its forests and woodlots are gone. We have turned forests into suburbs and meadows into malls. The trails once used by wildlife are now four lanes of pavement which we hurdle down at seventy miles an hour as we travel to a theatre or ball park which used to be swampland, but has since been drained and filled in order to build upon.

As the forests dwindled and the vast wilderness disappeared, so did the predators. Now, man has to assume the responsibility of managing the herds. We have to become stewards of the land. If the herds go unchecked without man as a predator they will in a few short years be so high in number that they will exterminate themselves through disease and starvation. The land can only hold and feed a certain number. Any more than that and a whole herd suffers. For example, imagine taking a dozen cows and fencing them in a small area. Provide them only enough food for six cows. Do this for six months and I doubt any of them will be around to see the seventh.

Aldo Leopold wrote in *A Sand County Almanac* the following lines representing the role of the wolves: "I now suspect that just as a deer herd lives in mortal fear of its wolves, so does the mountain live in mortal fear of its deer. And perhaps with better cause, for while a buck pulled down by wolves can be replaced in two or three years, a range pulled down by too many deer may fail of replacement in as many decades. Only the mountain has lived long enough to listen objectively to the howl of the wolves."

If we remove the wolves and other predators from the circle of life and fail to replace them, then we will be creating dust bowls by overpopulating, and the rivers will wash their future to the sea. I believe man must pick up where the wolves left off and cull the herds. Yes, man has the right to hunt and man has an obligation to control the wildlife population because our so-called progress has eliminated the predators that used to do that very thing.

First Hunts

When it came time to take my boys hunting for the first time, and they were allowed to carry a firearm and shoot at game, I drew from my experience. I remembered how my grandfather made me stay out there after I shot that first rabbit and how we had to take another one before we could go home. Then he made me help clean it and eat it. He knew what he was doing by keeping me out there instead of running away from what I had just done. I learned an important lesson about the taking of a life that day. It's not automatic; if the shot is not well-placed, death does not always come in an instant. If the aim is off, then there may be noises and movements that accompany death that one does not find comforting. Sometimes this can weigh heavy on a conscience, especially the first few times, and it should. Taking a life should be very personal and as hunters, we should do everything in our power to see that it's done quickly.

The first few times I took my sons out hunting, I would always take a different firearm, or at least a different size shot. Then when a shot presented itself, we would both shoot and this would leave them an out if the kill would bother them. It seems that I would always miss and they would always hit what we were shooting, and I would congratulate them on a fine shot. If I saw that it was bothering them, then upon cleaning the animal, we would soon discover that it was my shot that ended its life, or at least helped. This would help alleviate the blame that was weighing so heavy on their young hearts. And it did on more than one occasion.

Those days have long passed but I am blessed with several memories. I am thankful for the time spent with each of them, although it was not nearly enough. There is still that feeling though, that which accompanies the death of an animal and leaves a bit of sadness behind. I feel that should always be there and is a big part of being a responsible hunter. This taking of life is not a game and should not be just for bragging rights. If one feels that way, then they need to take a look inside themselves and figure it out, for we should be stewards of the land and not just killers. As hunters, we have a responsibility to keep the numbers in check, not just a license to kill.

The Trespasser

It was November 15, the opening day of Michigan's firearm deer season. I was looking forward to it as I do every year, and as usual, it took way too long to get here. I was up north at our family tent camp like every year, yet my mind was back home on my property. For the first week of the season, I have always hunted in northern Michigan; and to this day, I have never experienced an opener on my home turf. My wife's grandfather, Howard, would be hunting my property in my absence and I was excited for him. I had passed up a couple of small six-points and a tight racked eight during bow season. I had seen them several times and knew they were using my woods as a bedding area. I had several food plots they were using regularly.

I had instructed Howard to sit where I knew they were traveling. It was inside a huge hollowed-out maple tree. There was plenty of room to sit comfortably and be concealed from all directions. Someone years ago had cut out a window in the back side to watch the field where the food plots were. It provided protection from the wind and rain or snow, and it was quite cozy.

Howard was getting up there in age but he loved the deer woods so much that he needed to get out. If you love the wild world as much as Howard did then you will understand that need, that longing that pulls at your inner core. I had offered him our woods and promised he would be the only one out there. He would not be too far from the house if there were any problems. He promised to call my brother-in-law if he needed help getting a buck out of the woods. So, everything was set and I was excited for him. It had been awhile since he took a buck and he was really looking forward to it.

When opening morning dawned, Howard was right where I had told him to sit. He was filled with excitement and looking forward to seeing some antlers. With the eastern sky turning pink and the first rays of light reaching the forest floor, there came movement. In the distance, he could see two deer feeding their way toward him. He got his gun up on his knee and was ready if one was sporting antlers. As they came closer, he could see that their heads were bald, but one was really interested in her back-trail. They passed a mere twenty yards away without any idea he was sitting there in that hollow tree. A few minutes later, a small four-point came by with his nose to the ground. Howard let it pass to chase after the does. A few more minutes had passed when he saw a larger deer working the same trail. As it got closer, it stopped and started raking a small tree with its antlers. It was still about a hundred yards away and he didn't want to chance a shot. If it followed along the trail of the others, the deer would come within twenty yards and Howard then felt comfortable with the shot.

The buck left the small sapling and started down the trail a few yards. He then locked up and stood staring off to the south. Suddenly, he spun, and in a rush, headed back the way he came. Howard then heard some crashing to his right and turned his attention to the noise. It was just a few seconds before another hunter came into view. He was headed straight for Howard and walked right up to the tree. Howard said good morning and asked if the hunter might be lost. The man told him he was in his spot. He said the owner of the property had told him he could sit there and he was already late getting into the woods. Howard, being the kind-hearted man he was, got up and headed back to the house, not wanting to spoil someone else's hunt. He was, however, assuming I had told the other man that he could hunt there.

Howard had no longer reached my yard when he heard shooting and saw a buck run from the woods and down in the fencerow. It was a tight racked eight-point. The man ran over to the buck, grabbed an antler, pulled it down the fencerow, and put it in his truck and left. He didn't even stop to gut it out, which Howard thought was strange. Figuring the morning was ruined, Howard headed home. Since he thought I'd given someone else permission, he wanted to stay out of the way and he didn't go back. In fact, that would be the last time Howard would get out hunting.

[125]

As Howard relayed what happened that morning, he was genuinely happy for the hunter whom he thought was a friend of mine. To this day, I do not know who that man was. The only thing I know for sure is that he was a trespasser. He came on to my land without permission and kicked off the only person who had a right to be there. He stole something that day. Not so much from me, but from Howard. He stole Howard's hunt; he stole the joy he felt that morning as the sun was coming up and the woods was coming alive. He stole Howard's peace of mind, and he not only stole Howard's hunt, he stole Howard's last hunt. The day that was supposed to be special to him was ruined.

I cannot to this day understand how someone could be so heartless as to kick a gentle soul like Howard off of property that he himself had no business being on. I wish I would have been home that opening day, but at the same time, I'm glad I wasn't. I don't know what I would have done when I saw Howard coming up to the house and heard that shot that should have been his. I'm not the type to go out and pick a fight, but I will stick up for what is right and just. I knew that Howard's hunts were numbered and I'm sure I would have met that hunter before he ever got to his downed buck. It would not have been a pleasant confrontation.

Howard is not the kind of person who would complain, but I know that feeling to some extent. Although they were not my last hunts, trespassers have stolen many and left me feeling robbed. I would leave early from work so I could be in my tree early enough, only to find some trespasser had beaten me there. My woods, my tree stand, but someone else's butt in it.

That is what gets my dander up. I go to great lengths to keep my stands scent free. Nothing gets me more heated than to get to my tree stands that I have left alone until the wind was right, and then found evidence of someone else. Cigarette butts, pop bottles, beer cans, and trash in and around my stands, along with enough scent to ward off every deer in the county. I have had twenty-five pound mineral blocks carried off, not in some whitetail's backpack or by some squirrel with a tiny quad, but by trespassers. I have gone to the woods in the spring to hunt for mushrooms, only to find a patch of stems where someone else had already been. Someone who somehow missed the bright yellow *No Trespassing* signs every fifty feet along my property lines. I have found gut piles in front of my hunting shacks and empty shotgun slug shells inside them. I've found all of this and more from unwanted thieves with very little respect for others' property. Who knows, if they would have stopped and asked permission, we might be good friends today,, and even enjoy hunting together. But, they made a conscious choice to do otherwise.

So, if you are a trespasser or a violator, I'm sorry you wasted your money on this book. I'm sure you don't understand the parts about ethics or morals or integrity and character. If you would like your money returned, just send it back and I will gladly refund your money because this book was not written for you. It was written for true sportsmen and sportswomen, not slobs. If you are the one who was trespassing that opening day and spoiled Howard's last hunt, please come to my door and I will personally give your money back . . . right upside your head!

October Frost

There is still an hour or more of predawn darkness before the eastern horizon will begin to lighten. I have donned three layers of clothing and my face is painted to help me blend into the tree that will be my hiding spot for the next few hours. I zip up my Scentlock, put on my hat and gloves, grab my daypack and my bow, and I'm out the door. A rush of cold air fills my lungs as I greet the morning and I can see my breath in the darkness. There is a hard frost that the night brought and it feels wonderful beneath my rubber boots. The crunch of an October frost under my feet gives me the same joy, as best I can tell, as does warm sand between my wife's toes on some Caribbean beach.

The walk to my blind is silent because I raked a path to it a few days ago, and is done in total darkness so that the wandering beam of a flashlight does not give away my approach. I climb silently into my tree stand, put on my safety belt, and then pull up my bow and hang it where I can reach it should a shooter buck wander near my ambush spot. I make all the necessary adjustments to myself and my gear so the next few hours can be sat in total silence with very limited movement. I draw pants into boots, pull sleeves down over gloves, and tuck layers inside my beltline, all in an effort to keep out the cold that always seems to seek out bare skin. Finally, I take out a razor-sharp arrow and place it on my bow. A rush of excitement warms me and all my daily stresses temporarily leave my mind as I lean back against the red oak that has seen many, many, more Octobers than me. I close my eyes and begin each hunt as I always do with a soft, "Thank you Father for this beautiful morning and this beautiful woodlot with all its creatures and landscapes. Thank you for giving me each and every hour that I get to spend here. I am truly blessed. Guide my arrow true or let me miss completely, for the choice is up to you. Amen."

The magical hour is almost here and I eagerly, yet silently, await it, hearing nothing but my heartbeat in total anticipation of what is to come. As the eastern sky begins to lighten, the leaves rus-

A gentle breeze moves across the weed
the rows of corn, and then fills the woods.
ents of autumn—the smell of acorns and
rn; the woodsy hint of decaying leaves; the
rth and a touch of tarsal gland from the buck
a nearby scrape the night before. I inhale deeply and
draw a breath of October into my lungs. I hold it for a moment
and let it seep into the empty spaces of my soul. It supercharges
me.

Suddenly, I am a part of a grander scheme of things. I am much
more alert. The silence of the woods is amazing. My ears search
for the slightest crunch of a fallen leaf, or the crack of a twig,
anything that might portray the presence of an approaching
buck. The gentle breeze swirls about the forest and passes by
my nostrils. Twice more I smell tarsal glands; the second time
seems stronger. My nose is working overtime now. My mind is
silently trying to decipher the wind's direction and the source of
these exciting odors. It's playing tricks on me. A stick breaks
here, a leaf crunches there. Did I just hear a buck grunt? No, all
is silent. My imagination is making my mind wander and I be-
gin to daydream of the buck that haunts this woodlot. I have yet
to see the dominant buck in this area, but I have seen the dam-
age he has done to several trees. I have found his scrapes where
he has tore up the earth and left his scent, and the track that he
places in that scrape is the size of an elk's. I know he is noctur-
nal and moves only at night; that's how he got so old. But I also
know that an estrous doe can weaken his defenses and cause
him to make a mistake that just might bring him within range of
my bow. If this should happen, then I will be put to the test—the
months of practice, the placement of the stand. Can I keep from
shaking so badly that I give away my presence? Will I have the
strength to draw my bow? All of this and so much more comes
into play at that very moment. Will I be prepared? Only time
will tell.

The eastern sky is brighter now and darkness begins to fade into
shadows. The breeze picks up a bit and seems to breathe life

into the woodlot as leaves begin to rustle and a few trees begin to sway. Now the creatures of the forest begin to stir. First comes the call of a distant crow that is quickly answered by a lone gobbler. Then a scratchy remark from a fox squirrel that sounds a little testy, as if to say, "Shut up you fools. It's early yet."

A feisty red squirrel quickly answers the fox squirrel as if to say, "You're not so big. I can take you."

And then, the next few minutes are like a wildlife concert as the forest awakens and the woodlot comes alive. It's not long before the squirrels are on the forest floor in search of breakfast, and soon other birds and critters do the same.

I have waited nine long months for this morning. Ever since my last hunt on New Year's, I have been thinking of this day and how big the bucks I let walk last year would be this fall. The three-and-a-half-year-old eight-point that I drew on last year was a special concern of mine as I had yet to see him since May. Was he still alive and would he haunt my woodlot again when the does were ripe? Would he again wander past my ambush site blinded by his lust for the doe he was following? And would I again be able to draw my bow without detection? If this all came together, I just might release an arrow; and with my Maker's guidance, zip through his boiler room and take home a trophy worthy of naming a mature buck. He would be four-and-a-half this fall and he didn't get that old by being careless.

There is a sense of urgency about the forest now that I hadn't noticed even a couple weeks ago while hanging stands. The frost last night seems to have driven home the fact that seasons are a changing. This is the season of preparation and it will soon give way to the cold, biting north winds that are a prelude of winter. Only the fittest will survive and those who have the nec-essary fat built up, or a large storage of nuts, will stand a better chance of making it through until spring. I have planted a couple acres of corn and beans and left them standing just to help the animals through. The time and energy and the money spent to plant and grow these crops is all but paid for by just being able to be here this morning.

As the sun begins to break the horizon, the very tallest trees begin to reveal their colors that previously seemed to be lost in the darkness. At first just the tallest treetops are alive with color, and then as if an artist were taking horizontal strokes with a giant brush. The colors move slowly downward until they reach the forest floor and the whole woodlot comes alive with the vivid colors of October. The scarlet of maple, the dark red oak, the yellow of poplar, and the many shades of orange, paint a picture that the best of artists could not do justice. As the trees shed their colors, they drift silently to the ground or are lifted upward into the blue autumn skies where gentle breezes help to usher in the new season that is trying so hard to come early. This is Michigan in her finest hour; I wish time could stop here, in this season of the hunt.

I am taking in the autumn beauty when I hear the unmistakable rustle of footsteps in new fallen leaves. I turn my head ever so slowly in the direction of the sounds and see a pair of coyotes approaching. They are on a deer trail, which if they continue down it, will bring them within twenty yards of my stand. I slowly get to my feet, grab my bow, and turn so that I might take a shot if the chance presents itself. They keep coming down the trail and I ready myself for a shot. The coyotes have taken several small dogs in the neighborhood and I have often found their tracks in my yard. We have a couple small dogs of our own that belong to my mother-in-law, so she made me promise I will shoot any troublemakers I can as long as they are in season.

I place my fingers on the string and am about to draw when I hear rustling behind me. I slowly turn in that direction and there he is. A beautiful buck is not ten yards away. I don't count points because I don't want to get too nervous, but I do notice he has a lot of mass. He's probably a four-year-old. He freezes behind a couple of trees and his eyes are on the pair of coyotes as they pass, uninterested in his presence. I let them go by and focus my attention on the buck. What a beauty he is. He stands there behind the trees for what seems like an eternity. He doesn't move a muscle as he watches the coyotes until they are out of sight. The same can't be said of me; however, as my legs begin to shake and my breaths become shorter, my heartbeat is racing and adrenalin is pumping through my veins like water through a fire hose. The buck turns and looks in my direction. He then moves back around and walks straight away with the trees between us. He is gone almost as quickly as he appeared.

What an awesome morning. Already I've seen a pair of coyotes and a shooter buck, and it's early yet. As the morning plays out, I see several doe and a spike buck, unaware that a predator lurks above him, that gives me many shot opportunities while he scrounges for acorns beneath the very tree I am in. I draw a couple of times just for the practice and to see if I can do it undetected. I then watch as he feeds away.

The forest has quieted down by late morning and the warming rays of the sun threaten to lull me off to sleep. When the last of the deer are out of sight, I climb down from my stand. I silently leave the woodlot and as I am walking back to my house, I wander near the creek and see the slow moving water with leaves floating downstream. I notice how the tannin from the leaves that have fallen have stained the water and turned its color to a browner hue. I think autumn too has stained my being. It has left me with a taste of a simpler world that our forefathers experienced, a longing to spend every hour of my day in the fall woods, engaged in the hunt that is only a sport to me, but a way of life for them. I have a yearning for simpler times and often think I was born two hundred years too late. As I near my house I hear an automobile on the road and I am slapped back to reality; but hey, it's only October and I still have lots more chances to hunt. There is a shooter buck that uses my woods and I hope to see him again.

I am truly blessed. Thank you, Father.

The Blood Trail

The third week of October in 2002 found my hunting companions and I on a bow hunt in the western half of Michigan's Upper Peninsula. The weather had been warm and we were hoping the cold front they had promised would move in to cool the air off and heat the deer movement up. The hunting had been slow with sightings far and few between. A bumper crop of acorns kept the bucks from moving about too much and the rut was still a couple weeks away. I found a nice pine I was comfortable in and it overlooked a couple oaks and a few nice scrapes. There was a lot of sign in the area and it butted up to a bunch of private land that hadn't been hunted yet this season. I felt very confident in my stand location, even though a main road was only a hundred yards behind me. On the way into camp a few days earlier, we had spotted a nice buck on the edge of the road. It was on state land so I could hunt there. The next morning we found several rubs and scrapes in the area so my excitement was high and I couldn't wait for the wind to be right to hunt it.

Three days passed before the conditions were right and what a morning that was. We woke up to four inches of wet snow and the perfect wind for that stand. I overdressed and sucked down a cup of coffee on the way out. Even though the ground was white, it was still plenty dark when I climbed into my stand. The cold was welcome and the freeze the night before promised to turn the deer on and the mosquitoes off. The morning was dead still and as the eastern sky started to brighten, I heard a coyote yelp, followed by a few ravens that scolded him for breaking the silence.

I reached into my backpack to pull out a pair of gloves and when I sat back upright, I saw movement out in front of me. As I stared in that direction ,I could see a deer's shape materialize. I then realized it was the buck I had seen a few days ago. He stood there for the longest time, staring in my direction, and then put his head down to eat a few acorns. After a few minutes, he lifted his head and stared in my direction before starting to walk straight towards me. I could hear a car coming down the road a ways off and said a prayer that it wouldn't send him running for cover. The buck was about sixty yards out and closing the distance with every step. He was looking directly under me at the road and listening to that car as it neared. He stopped at about twenty yards and stood watching the road until the car passed by. Then he started to turn broadside, finally offering me a shot. He turned to look behind him and I drew my bow without standing up. Then my legs began to shake with excitement and the whole tree started to shake. He whipped his head around and stared right at me. I slowly lifted my feet up off the stand and the tree stopped shaking. He seemed to be looking right through me and I could hear my heart trying to pound its way through my chest. I slowly lowered my feet to the stand and the tree started to shake once again. I lifted them back up and the whole time, the buck is staring a hole through me. He turned his head and looked away for a second; I lined up my pin on his sweet spot. I was having trouble holding back the string and figured this was my chance. I relaxed my fingers and as I released, I rocked forward thrusting my arm down. I watched in frustration as my arrow disappeared through the buck, eight inches to the left of where I was aiming. No lungs there, only liver, and I cursed myself for not planting my feet. The buck spun around, ran straight away, and disappeared into the woods.

I sat there for a few minutes and then got down and picked up my arrow. The color of the shaft reinforced my thoughts and I knew I was in for a long track. I was so mad that I decided not to wait for my ride and walked back to the lodge to discuss my hit with a buddy. It was a two mile walk back to camp and I relived that shot over and over a hundred times in my head, every time getting madder at myself for releasing that arrow. Damn it! I knew better. I got back to camp and explained my blunder to the three guys who were still there. We decided to give it a couple hours and figured with the fresh snow, we wouldn't have any trouble picking up the trail.

We got back to my stand about 11 a.m. and sorted out the tracks, finally picking up a slight blood trail to follow. The sun was out and the snow was rapidly melting as we tracked. After about four hundred yards, we came across a fresh gut pile and I was sure someone had taken my buck. There were tracks everywhere and then my buddy yelled, "I have blood over here and a large track. I don't think that's your deer."

The tracks went in every direction with no rhyme or reason, like thoughts coming apart as they so often do when you don't write them down and they go by way of the wind. It's that curse of aging that leaves you scratching your head and asking yourself, *What was I just thinking?* We started off on the largest track and soon found a fresh bed with blood in it. We were sure we had jumped it, so we sat down and waited for about twenty minutes before we started off again. The blood was scarce and we would go twenty to thirty yards before we would find another drop. We had gone another two hundred yards when we jumped a deer and saw it run off. We checked its bed to realize it was definitely the one we were after. We sat down again and waited for another thirty minutes. We picked back up on the trail and soon were into an area where tracks went everywhere. We each went off on a set of tracks until someone came across a drop of blood. We were back on course. Drops of blood were farther apart now, and finally there were no more. We stayed on that track and again jumped a deer. As it ran off, I could see its head and knew it was my buck. This time I noticed it was having trouble running. We sat down again for a few minutes and then pushed on. After about three hundred more yards, I saw a deer lying next to some brush on the edge of the river. I had my buddies stand there for a moment and I stalked closer. I then had them start walking at an angle parallel to the deer. As they did, the deer followed them with his eyes and I was able to get into a position where I could send an arrow where it should have gone in the first place.

In ten seconds it was all over and we were staring down at my nicest buck ever. My buddies wanted to shake my hand but I said I didn't deserve it. They walked down the riverbank as I dressed the deer and came back shortly saying we were only a hundred yards from the lodge. It was four in the afternoon when we started dragging my buck towards the lodge. We pulled it up on the pole and as I stood back and admired it, I thanked the Lord again, this time for giving me companions who refused to give up even when it looked like there was no hope of finding it.

It was as I walked up the stairs to my room and began to change my clothes, that I noticed my legs were heavy. My body ached all over but I was aglow with personal satisfaction that we pushed on. I didn't celebrate that night because the shot I made did not warrant it. I did, however, toast to three great friends for sticking with me, for pushing me, and for understanding how sick I felt that the deer was out there suffering from a misplaced arrow that never should have been released until my shot was steady. I realized then how fortunate I am to have hunting partners who have the type of conviction these guys do.

Steve, Doug, and Rick: I am forever grateful, and I hope you know that I will be the first to pick up the trail if any of you are ever in that pinch. My hope is that I never take our friendship for granted. I am proud to call you guys my hunting partners, for you are the epitome of true sportsmen and I am blessed to be included in your camps. Thank you.

Bigfoot, Big Bears, Big Bucks, and Fishermen

It was the third week of October in 1992 and we were bow hunting up north in God's country east of Grayling, Michigan, near the town of Luzern. I was still wearing my camo after the morning hunt and was just getting out of my truck in town to grab a soda when I noticed the little berg was alive with activity. The streets were full of tourists, a couple news' crews, and writers and photographers. I figured out what all the fuss was about when a reporter stuck a microphone in my face and asked if I had seen Bigfoot? I laughed it off, said, "You have got to be kidding," and then stepped around him to go in and get my pop. Inside the store, I read the newspaper headline: *Bigfoot Spotted on Seven Occasions.*

Great, I thought. Now there would be more goofballs in the woods. Last year it was anti-hunters and now Sasquatch had come to visit. It was probably another ploy to get more people walking around in the woods to spoil our hunting. The newspaper said that the sightings had all been in the last few days, so I thought it strange that every store already had a rack full of t-shirts that said *Luzern, Home of Bigfoot*. I have in the past had shirts made up for my ball teams and not once were they done in less than two weeks; but hey, stranger things have happened.

I went back to camp and had lunch with the gang. We had a very deep discussion (well, as deep as it gets for us yahoos) about the large hairy creature that had invaded our hunting grounds. We had a couple of new hunters with us that year and they were not as sure as we were that the giant monster didn't exist. And so, the guys played up the hype and soon we could see a hint of belief in their eyes. There was that half eaten carcass found up in that tree last year and they did find that calf on top of that farmer's silo just a mile west of here. Only a man-like creature could climb those steps up the side. I did hear that ungodly scream coming from somewhere deep in the swamp just before the sun came up this morning. And don't forget that gal they found unconscious in the woods, the one who later gave

[137]

birth to that baby that was covered with hair. The one who, by the way, made the cover of the *National Inquirer* or something or other. Yeah, all of a sudden everybody had some recollection of a close encounter of the third kind.

We finished our discussion and headed back out to our blinds. I dropped both new hunters off at their spots and then went on to my own stand. For the sake of anonymity, we'll call these hunters BJ and Chief. I was hunting about a mile away from BJ and maybe five hundred yards away from Chief.

My stand was set so it overlooked some oaks and was situated in a large pine tree, being very well concealed. This night I was trying a string tracker on my bow because the swamp behind me was so thick and wet and I didn't want to lose an animal. I had never used a tracker before, other than while practicing, so it promised to be an interesting hunt. I was on a mission to get some venison in the freezer and be able to concentrate on a mature buck, so I elected to take a big doe if the chance presented itself. The gentle breeze died down, stillness set in, and all was quiet as the evening approached. There is a type of silence in the north woods along those cedar swamps that sort of pushes in on you; it's so quiet that it's almost noisy. I could still hear the does as they approached from quite a distance and made their way out of the swamp through the overgrown cut and up into the oaks in front of me. The one to the rear was quite large and I elected to take her if she allowed me with a double lung shot. After what seemed like several hours, but was probably only fifteen minutes, she wandered down by me. When she turned broadside, I put my pin on the sweet spot and released my string. The arrow found its target and she spun and headed straight away with line in tow. The string was whipping out of the spool just like a salmon making a run. Without even thinking, I yelled out "Fish on."

Within just a few seconds, the line stopped moving and I knew she was down for good. I was packing up my stuff when I heard my buddy Steve whistle. I returned the whistle and he met me at the bottom of my tree. He said he heard me shoot as he was walking up the trail and wondered if I got a good hit. He had also shot one, but it went into a thick area and he lost the blood and wondered if I would come help track it. I thought mine would be easy to find after dark by just following the string so I of course was happy to go help retrieve his.

We returned to his blind where he climbed back the tree and re-lived the shot. Soon we were off in the right direction and then busy dragging out another fat doe for the freezer. By the time we got back to his truck, it was dark. So on the way back to my blind we stopped to pick up BJ. As we pulled up on the road out front of his blind and tooted the horn, the prankster in me reared its ugly head.

I climbed out the window so the dome light wouldn't come on and then I ran into the woods to hide along the trail. I could hear BJ walking out. Why the fact that he was wearing a cast from the knee down to mend a broken foot never dawned on me then, still amazes me. My placement and timing could not have been more perfect and as he passed just a few feet away, I reached out and grabbed his leg. I let out a growl that sent him on a dead run towards the truck. At that point, the fact that he had the cast on was driven into in my thick skull every time BJ stepped down and let out a loud "Ouch. Ouch, ouch, ouch, ouch," all the way to the road. As I write this, it seems funny; but as I made my way back to the truck, I knew there would be hell to pay and I was practicing my apologies. As a new guy to camp, BJ took it in good stride but I soon would find out that he wasn't the only one a little hot under the collar.

Steve took me back to my truck, gave his keys to BJ so he could go pick up Chief, and then Steve and I retrieved my deer. When we got back to camp and were hanging up our deer, Chief seemed to be a little upset. Upon further investigation, we dis-covered he had a very nice nine-point buck with a drop tine over his right eye, coming into his apple pile, along with several does. "The does were eating the apples beneath my stand and the buck was within range, but hadn't yet offered a broadside shot, when some damn fisherman in the swamp laid into a fish and yelled, 'Fish on.' Then, he later carried on quite a conversation with his fishing buddy and scared every deer in the county deep into the swamps."

We told him we felt sorry for him but hadn't heard any fishermen ourselves and it must have been Bigfoot trying his luck at fly-fishing. Chief caught a lot of grief about what he saw and why he didn't get a shot if he had time to count tines. They told him there were no fishable waters close to where he was hunting and he might want to see a specialist when he returned home. He held to his story none-the-less.

That night, we ate fresh venison, swapped stories, kidded Chief, and played cards. The next afternoon found us back in the woods and again the evening was dead quiet. I had dropped BJ off at a different stand with a shorter walk. For some odd reason his foot was a little swollen. Chief was still too upset and chose not to hunt because of the damn fishermen. I chose a different stand deeper in the cedar swamp and as the night played out, I saw a few does and one small buck in the distance, but never picked up my bow. I was looking for a mature buck now. I had meat in the freezer and it was time to get serious.

Deep in the swamp the night comes early, and light fades quickly as the sun nears the horizon. The last rays of light ricocheted off the tallest of the treetops and the shade crept in slowly. Then it rushed in and choked out all remaining light on the forest floor. The autumn sky looked lonesome and turned from red, to purple, to black. The sky had clouded up and snowflakes began to fall. The forest took on a much less friendly atmosphere as the temperature dropped and the wind picked up. rattling the leaves that still remained in the treetops. The woods was silent now, void of any bird and squirrel chatter . Then, a lone coyote broke the silence. A shiver, caused either by the onset of colder temperatures or the coyotes plea, shot down my back. It really didn't matter the cause because I knew it was time to leave this place. A warm cabin awaited me along with the camaraderie of close friends and relatives., and the possibility that someone might have scored and have a buck to collect. I made my way back to the truck and picked up BJ, who told me he got a shot on a deer and didn't think it had gone far. Just then, my brother pulled up and said he shot a buck and needed help tracking it. It had started to snow pretty hard so we elected to go find my brother's buck first as BJ had heard his go down and knew where it was. What we thought would be an easy task took several hours to sort with all the falling snow. We did manage to find his six-point and loaded it in the truck. Everyone was wet and cold so we chose to go get BJ's deer in the morning. There was talk that Bigfoot could approach pretty close to a man without him hearing because his footsteps would be muffled in the snow, but I'm sure that had nothing to do with the decision to stay in camp.

We celebrated the buck and played cards, and then got up the next morning to go fetch a deer. When we got to BJ's stand, he climbed up and relived the shot. We found the spot where the deer should have been, but it was gone. We would soon discover that a large sow black bear and her cub had drug it off into the swamp. We followed it for a ways and when the swamp got really thick, we decided it wouldn't be such a good idea to take on an angry sow protecting her cub and her dinner, just to recover a half-eaten deer . . . especially since no one was armed. All our bows were back at camp. Bears one, hunter zero.

The next day was pretty quiet and then we left for home. My brothers and I, along with my cousins, returned three weeks later to set up camp for the rifle season. On opening day, from the same stand Chief had been in, my cousin took a fine nine-point with a drop tine over his right eye. But, no fishermen were heard on this trip. We decided not to tell Chief about the buck or the fishermen; some things are best left unsaid. We got three more bucks that trip and before we left, we gave in to the tourist trap and all went home with shirts that said: *Luzern, Home of Bigfoot.*

[141]

The Drag

November 15' 2007 found me, like any other opener, nestled in my blind well before first light. I had dropped my two sons off at their blinds on the way into mine. They were both hunting the high ground close to camp so if the cold got the better of them, they could go back and warm up. Me, I was planning on sitting until dark unless I got lucky.

The mercury dipped below freezing, but I was plenty warm because the walk in had gotten me heated up. I loaded my rifle, racked in a shell, and set it aside where I could reach it if an opportunity presented itself. I grabbed my thermos, poured a hot cup of coffee, and sat back in anticipation of what first light would bring. We were hunting the upper part of Michigan's lower peninsula and I was hunting down in an old cedar swamp.

As I sat and enjoyed the peacefulness, my mind drifted back to this same swamp some thirty plus years ago when I first started hunting with my uncles. The parts I remembered most were the drags. When someone shot a deer deep in the swamp, it was always a half day's work getting it out. It was hard work, but I always enjoyed it, sometimes pushing myself too hard, trying to prove that I too, was a man. The swamp was always wet and muddy because the beavers had a notion to make it a lake. There were fallen trees and blow-downs everywhere, and it really was a mess to negotiate while dragging a deer behind you. It was hard work but very rewarding, and whenever anyone would mention deer camp, they always brought up the drag. It was a highlight to us younger hunters. Those uncles have been gone for over twenty years and now we are up here with our kids and soon some of our grandkids. Only my brother and I still hunt the swamp, and the drag from the swamp has become a rarity.

One of the regulars in camp was my cousin Jim who fell victim to a hunting accident last fall and was killed. As our uncles had, he left a huge void in our camp that can never be replaced. As I sat there thinking of him and the hunts and drags we shared, I shed a few tears and began to think about his three boys who still hunted with us. They grew up hunting with their dad and shared many a hunt and drag, but if I were to ask them, I know they would all say it was nowhere near enough. Thinking of Jim and his boys, my mind drifted to my own sons. This was the first year that I had both of them at camp at the same time. They were grown men, yet we had never shared a drag from the swamp. Something that had meant so much to me, and I hadn't yet shared it with them. I felt I had cheated them out of a large part of what deer camp was about. It's not the killing we go to camp for, it's what comes before and after that counts. It's the camaraderie and bonding that makes memories worth mounting in your mind. That's the true reason we go north. There are more deer and bigger bucks in my own woods, if that's what I was after. But that's not where the real memories are made. I wanted a story my boys could pass on, not just a dusty old head-mount. I wanted a memory worth saving. I wanted the drag.

As first light came and went, I saw a couple doe and then all was quiet. Again, my mind wandered to past hunts and time spent with loved ones. I recalled all the lunch breaks I used to spend with Jim when we shared the swamp, as well as the drags we shared and how much I enjoyed his company. I wished he were here for one more drag. Then, I began to think how his life was cut short; there would be no more drags with his boys. At that moment, I realized I was not invincible myself. If I passed on this next year, I would never have given my sons the pleasure of the drag. In deep thought, I drifted off to sleep in the stillness of the swamp and my dreams were filled with past hunts.

I have no idea how long I slept, but I was awakened to what I thought was someone whispering my name. I looked around and saw no one, but movement in front of me caught my eye. A buck materialized out of the blow-downs and stood just twenty yards in front of me. He turned and looked away and I heard a voice whisper, "the drag." My gun came up, I fired, and the buck was dead. I sat there for several minutes as a rush of emotions passed through me. Then I wiped my eyes and walked over to where he lay. I knelt down and stroked his head and thanked my Creator for this prize. The walk back to camp was shorter than I recalled, for there was a bounce in my step. My boys were already at camp warming up and I relayed the good news—they were about to go on a drag.

They seemed less than enthusiastic and were slow getting around. We got back to my blind, dressed the deer, and started out with it. It was slow going and I realized just how out of shape I was. Despite the cold, we all worked up a good sweat and both sons swore they were going to have a heart attack if we didn't have a break every hundred feet. They were griping and complaining the whole way, and I was loving it. They kept asking me why I was smiling and what was so funny. I just kept smiling because I knew someday they would remember the drag. They would remember the times we spent together and hopefully, would want to pass it on to their children.

I didn't need that deer that day; I had one in the freezer from a previous bow hunt. What I did need, however, was that memory. Not so much for me, but more so for them. Was I selfish taking another buck? Maybe, but the meat won't go to waste. I'll eat every bite with a smile on my face as I remember those boys huffing and puffing and complaining about how their arms and backs hurt and telling me. They warned me that I better not shoot another one down in the swamp or I could drag it myself.

The rack was small but the memory is huge. It's a trophy worth hanging in my memory bank and hopefully one they will cherish later in their lives. When they think back to those first years at deer camp and they are sharing the memories with their sons, they will talk about the drag. Somewhere over time, they will forget about the strained muscles and the sore back and legs, and with any luck, will want to head deep into the cedar swamp. There they can hunt that elusive buck and with any luck bring home a trophy worth mounting in their minds.

The drag, how sweet it is.

The Empty Woods

October came too quickly in 2004. The days were growing shorter and cooler and I was not ready when bow season rolled around. It snuck up on me like a great horned owl swoops down on a snowshoe. All at once it's there and you can't do anything about it except chew yourself out for not being prepared. Any other year I would have been ready. Hundreds of arrows should have been launched through my bow, tree stands should have been up for several weeks by then, and all my camo should have been washed and hung out to dry a week ago. Something was different this year and I couldn't put my finger on it.

October 1st came and I was not ready. I was all over the target and I needed more time to zero in my bow. I shot as often as I could and I had it down by the seventh of October. I headed to the woods. I was not as excited as I usually would have been donning my camo and painted face. I walked out to the barn and grabbed my bow, flung a few practice arrows, and by 4 p.m., I was on my way to my stand. As I walked the edge of the corn-field, I passed by the stand my buddy used and it was then that I realized why it felt so differently. I was by myself on this hunt and would be on every hunt this year because he had moved to Michigan's Upper Peninsula. For the last twenty-four years, I had shared my hunts with this buddy and every one was a suc-cess, whether we took a shot or not. He shared the same code of ethics and the same love and respect for the whitetail as I did. He would gladly give up a hot stand to me for a colder one if he thought I might get a shot. I too found it more enjoyable to share in his success than in my own, for his excitement was both cap-tivating and contagious. It was a joy to share a hunt with him and all these years, I had taken that for granted. I knew he would always hunt as long as he drew a breath, but it never dawned on me that he would move so far away.

I used to feed off his excitement and we would practice to-gether. As the season grew nearer, we would place our stands out with each other's help and while one was up in the tree, the other would trim away shooting lanes. It was always the same, we would get to the tree where we were going to hang a stand and he would say, "Get up there monkey boy and hang it solid." I would hang it and then he would climb up and cut out the branches that were in his way. Our stands were always set up just the opposite as he was left-handed and I was right. And many times when using each others, we had to pass on a shot because the buck came in on the wrong side.

It was always nice to share a beer or a soda with him after each hunt and swap stories from the last few hours, or follow a blood trail and drag out a nice buck. I missed him already and this was only my first hunt of the season. We shared a bond that only hunting companions could begin to understand. We knew each other when it came to hunting whitetails and we thought alike. I knew that if he was not at our meeting spot on time that there were probably deer under his stand and he couldn't climb down. I would wander that way until I heard them run off and he could get down without being detected. As he walked up to me, I could tell by his pace if he had seen a shooter or if he had gotten a shot. I shared his excitement as he talked about that evening's hunt. I also shared his pain if he took a shot and didn't see the animal go down. It was that sickness in your stomach and the heavy feeling in your chest like someone was sitting on it. You start to doubt your shot placement and even your ability as a hunter. You know that these feelings will only go away when you walk up on the animal after a short blood trail. I knew if I made one of these shots and had an animal to track that he would be there and wouldn't give up until I was ready to call it a night. And, he would be right back in the morning if I asked.

I recalled a lot of the hunts we shared as I walked to the back of my woodlot, and as I passed another one of his stands, I saw the tree that still had one of his broad heads in it. He nailed it dead center, which would have been a perfect shot if we were hunting wild cherry and not the buck that stood on the opposite side of it. I chuckled to myself and thought how much I would miss hunting with him this fall. I got to my stand and climbed up without the usual excitement, for there was a loneliness in the air that evening.

I love the fall, the colors of red and orange on the trees, the corn dried out and the ears turned down, the thorn apples red on the trees, and the sound of falling acorns each time the wind blows. I like the cool air that is a welcome relief to the summer heat and helps drive away the mosquitoes that buzz around your face and threaten to give away your presence if you swat at them. The cool air brings with it a sense of urgency that is all too apparent in the activity of the squirrels. Those same squirrels who a month ago were more concerned with play now had a purpose to each movement they make. This is the season of preparation, and each creature knows it needs to bulk up or stock up to make it through the hard winter ahead.

All these things about fall that I so much liked were about me. It was a familiar place to me as I had owned and hunted these woods for many seasons past; yet there was a sense of loneliness about it this time that I remembered to well. It was there the years my uncles had passed on and no longer graced us with their presence at deer camp. I knew I would hunt with my buddy again at some point, yet the feeling still lingered and felt heavy in my chest as though I had suffered the loss of a dear friend. He hadn't passed away, but the companionship I so much looked forward to was gone, leaving an empty feeling in the air that echoed through the woods. I sat there for I don't how long, lost down memory lane as hunt after hunt paraded through my mind when all of a sudden a shooter buck materialized under my stand. Without thinking, I drew my bow, anchored my finger, and put the pin on the sweet spot behind his shoulder. I held there for a few seconds and then relaxed my string. This was a nice buck and I wanted to share the hunt. My sons would be home for Thanksgiving and my buddy said he might be down for the last week of December. I could wait. The buck gave me several more opportunities before he walked out of range, but I just couldn't bring myself to the task of taking his life.
Was I getting soft? No, I doubt it. I was just lonely for a friend

who I truly missed. All these years, I had taken for granted his friendship and the camaraderie that we shared. Being a man, it often goes unsaid how much we appreciate a true friend. But hey, I have broad shoulders and at risk of being a softy, can say: *Hey buddy, I miss our time in the woods and I miss your presence. I look forward to the next time we walk a wooded trail together on the way to our stands. I cherish the memories, wish you luck in the north woods, and maybe in our next telephone conversation, we can set the date in stone. Always stay downwind and shoot straight pal. And may a shooter come your way.*

A Camp on Higher Ground

I was on a gun hunt years ago
After a whitetail buck
Dressed for cold in Woolrich
I hoped to have good luck

The morning had dawned crisp and cold
With new snow on the ground
A thousand acres to myself
And nobody else around

I was camping in the north woods
Where my uncles used to stay
They'd leave their tent camp before light
And hunt the swamp all day

It was at this camp I learned so much
About the whitetail deer
And about a code of ethics
I'd use throughout the year

This morn the swamp was quiet
The cold bit at my skin
It wrestled with my buttons
Tried it's hardest to get in

A northern wind began to blow
And pushed the mercury down
Picking up new fallen snow
And blowing it around

I thought I must be crazy
To be sitting here today
My tent was warm with stove ablaze
Four hundred yards away

But then the eastern sky grew pink
The magic hour was near
The rising sun would bring daylight
And I might see some deer

So I brushed the snow off of my gun
And pulled my gloves up tight
And waited as the morning sun
Bid farewell to the night

As the sun peaked o'er the horizon
The cold wind ceased to blow
And the first rays chased the darkness
Across new fallen snow

The morning light brought beauty
Like I'd never seen before
I had not anticipated
What this morning had in store

The silence it was deafening
The air was cold and still
I was taking in the beauty
When I saw movement on the hill

Not a living creature
Just some movement in the trees
Coming down off of the ridge
And heading straight for me

And then a presence overwhelmed me
I no longer was alone
I felt spirits move about me
All free of flesh and bone

And then I felt God's breath upon me
Like a warm and gentle breeze
And I heard the hymns of autumn
In the rustling of the leaves

The hunter's choir joined in
With their sweet angelic sound
My uncle's voices were among those
From the camp on higher ground

A ray of sun broke through the cedars
And gently warmed my face
And I knew that very moment
Why they all so loved this place

It wasn't deer that they were chasing
It was answers to their life
A place to feel alive again
Free of life's cruel strife

The cold had left my body
I felt so warm and safe
I felt the souls of all my loved ones
Who had left this earthly place

I knew that they were with me
They came to say hello
And tell me of a better place
Where all God's children go

For there is a camp on higher ground
Somewhere beyond the ridge
And from the swamps of earthly pain
The Lord has built a bridge

I know that we can cross it
There's no way that we can fail
If only we believe it's true
That Christ has blazed the trail

I sat there taking in the beauty
And had just wiped away a tear
When out from behind a deadfall
A whitetail buck appeared

His face and back were black as coal
His neck, muscled thick and wide
Three hundred pounds if he's an ounce
At ten yards he stood broadside

I'd spent a lifetime searching
For a trophy such as he
But I never raised my gun up
Something had come over me

His beauty took my breath away
So majestic was his crown
King of the forest surely
I couldn't gun him down

I could see as he walked closer
Because not a bit of fear he showed
A cross-shaped scar upon his shoulder
Above a hole where crimson flowed

Beads of blood dripped down his antlers
His tracks filled with that same red
Dark eyes that stared right through me
No words needed to be said

I knew that was the king of kings
The ruler of this land

He came to me in a vision
In a way that I could understand

I'm not the sharpest in the tool shed
But that day I felt his pain
As he shared a bit of heaven
In a world that's so insane

Then he leapt over the deadfall
And vanished in thin air
Left me alone there in my refuge
From a world that doesn't care

I pondered the hour behind me
Were these old eyes playing tricks
Or was that another wake-up call
For this old hypocrite

That old swamp is my oasis
In this desert we call life
An island in life's ocean
Free of pain and strife

So I sat a while just taking in
The beauty of the snow
So different than the real world
Where Satin's tugging at your soul

Then I gathered up my rifle
And threw my compass in my pack
I saw true north in my vision
And now I knew the right way back

I broke camp and headed homeward
Left the cedar swamps behind
Rushed home to see my family
And hung a trophy in my mind

[153]

Just Sail

I've always had a liking for older people. They have so much knowledge because they've seen so much in their lifetimes. The older, the wiser, I think. Old Jack was no different, a little rough around the edges, maybe a little coarse at times, like sandpaper. He comes at you, rough at first, and then smoothes you into a friend. Years ago, my Grandma on my father's side told me to listen to my elders. There's always a lesson if you really listen, and not just with your ears. You have to listen with your heart. It may not be big, but a lesson just the same. So, I listened to Old Jack and he didn't disappoint me.

The first time I met Jack, the only time actually, was years ago during a motorcycle trip a buddy and I were taking around Lake Superior. We had a few hundred miles under us for the day and decided it was enough. It looked like rain up ahead so we stopped and got a room in a little harbor town. There were a few commercial fishing boats tied up at the docks and that seemed to be where all the action was. We were hungry so we stopped into the local tavern for a bite to eat and perhaps a cold one to wash away the road dust. The place was empty except for the tender behind the bar and a well-aged gentleman pulled up in front of it. We'd soon come to know him as Old Jack.

A sign behind the bar read, *Save a Fish, Spear an Indian*, and life-rings and old oars covered the walls, each bearing the name of a Great-Lakes' ship. Many of the oars and life rings had names written on them; I would soon learn from Old Jack that those were names of sailors lost, those who went to the bottom with their cargo in the icy waters of the Superior. It didn't take a rocket scientist to figure out that there was history here.

There were two more stools at the bar so we grabbed them and I sat down next to the one they called Old Jack. I offered up a hello and he turned and looked at me. His face was wrinkled and weathered from too many days in the wind, but his smile was inviting as he looked at me and said, "Kind of hairy, ain't ya?"

"What's that?" I said, and he repeated, "You're kind of hairy ain't you?"

"Yes, I guess I am," I said. " How you doing?"

"I'm fine" he said, "Name's Jack. What's that helmet for? You ain't no Hell's Angel are you?" I answered that I wasn't a Hell's Angel and then he asked, "You a troll? One of them apple knockers?"

"If you mean am I from down state; yes, I am. Are you an ornery old fart or just nosey?"

"Both," he said, "You one of them hippies from Detroit?" When I told him I wasn't a hippie either, Old Jack went on to explain, "That's Rat back there in the kitchen. We call him Rat on account of his ears. He climbed up some mooring line off a freighter years ago and I took a liking to him. But don't tell him I said that; he'll get all mushy on us. You gotta name?"

"It's Taylor," I said. "Can I buy you a drink?"

"Don't mind if you do," he said. "Rat, get out here and set us up. Say, you ain't one of those Taylors that make that Taylor's Whiskey are ya? Because I don't like that stuff. Sorry if you are."

When I told him I wasn't one of those Taylors, he said "Good. Rat get out here and set us up. You sleeping back there or you skinning road kill for supper?" The bartender came out of the kitchen and asked what we needed. Jack told him, "These boys and I need a drink, so set us up."

"What can I get you?" he asked.

My buddy replied that he didn't want anything and that he was heading back to the room. "Is he all right?" Jack asked. "He looks a little green around the gills."

[155]

"We got into some bad food up in Ontario yesterday and he still isn't feeling too good. That's part of the reason we stopped." And then to the bartender, "I'll take a coke and whatever Jack wants."

"Coming right up," he said, "The name's Rat . . . on account of the ears."

"Yeah, I heard. Also heard you crawled up a mooring rope and called this place home. The name's Taylor. Nice to meet you Rat."

Then Jack asked me if I'd do him a favor. He asked me if I would go over to the jukebox and play a couple songs. "Play B-7," he said, "and play it twice. Then you can play what you want for the third song. It's on me; here's a quarter. Make sure you don't play that B-6. I played that the other day by mistake. That stuff hurt my ears."

I took his quarter and went over to the jukebox to take a look. B-7 was Gordon Lightfoot, and B-6 was Michael Jackson's *Beat It*. Big difference, I thought. I played B-7 twice and then went back and sat down next to Old Jack. As *The Wreck of the Edmund Fitzgerald* started playing, Rat leaned over and turned the fan off and dimmed the light above the bar. Old Jack took off his hat and stared down at his drink. He never looked up until the song played through twice. That was one of my favorite songs, and I've heard it a hundred times. Yet, that was the first time I felt it, and I could see Jack was feeling it too. When he looked up, he had a tear on his cheek. "That's why Rat dims the light," he said, "so people don't see me crying. He's afraid I might scare off all these customers. You can go play your song now."

"I don't think I need to," I said. "I think that song said it all. We'll save one for later."

"Mighty nice of ya. Mighty nice of ya."

Just as Rat set our drinks on the bar, his wife walked in and said, "It's time to go Jack. The doctor's waiting, and if that's whiskey you got in front of you, he isn't going to be happy."

Jack slugged back his drink and said, "I'll be right back. If you're still here when I get back, I'll buy the next round."

"I'll be here," I replied. "Got nowhere to go until my buddy's feeling better."

"Good," he said, and out the door he went.

"Don't mind that old boy. He's harmless," Rat claimed. "His bark is worse than his bite, but he'll grow on you, just like an old barnacle."

"I kind of like him," I said. "He reminds me of someone."

"Must be good people," Rat said.

"He was. He sure was."

Rat started washing glasses in front of me and I asked him about B-7. "The song hits pretty close to home," he said. And with that came the story of Jack.

"Old Jack's father was a logger. He tried getting Jack into it, but Jack said the lake kept calling him. So he got a job on a freighter when he was just thirteen. He worked the freighters for thirty years and then after his brother died in a mine accident, he came back to work the fishing boats. He wanted to be close to his nephew as well as his great-nephew who he just called Junior. Junior was my best friend. Our fathers shipped out to Korea together and neither one of them came back. Old Jack took Junior in, and me as well. He called us his twins. He kept working the fishing boats so he could be home at night to take care of us. He liked the boats, but you could tell he longed to be back on the freighters. He would always tell us all these exciting stories.

[157]

As we grew up, we worked the docks and once and a while a boat would need a crewmember so we could go out. We saved our money, and Junior's dream was to get a commercial fishing boat of our own so all three of us could fish together. Jack thought we were missing out and told us we needed to try out the freighters for a year. Then if we still wanted to buy a boat, he'd do it. Jack had every intention of fishing with us; he even ordered the boat. It was going to take a year to build, but he wanted to surprise us so he never told Junior or me about it. I was engaged so I stayed in town and bought this bar. Jack got Junior a job on a freighter. Junior was onboard the day she went down. Just like the Edmund Fitzgerald, a November gale whipped up the lake and broke her in half. She went to the bottom with her crew. Jack has always blamed himself for Junior's death. He said it was him who talked Junior into it. Thinks he'd still be alive if he had let him buy that boat. 'Man's got a right to fish' he would say. Jack came off the water that week and hasn't been back out since. And he never did take delivery of that boat. He hit the bottle pretty hard for a few years. Drank so much he lost his eyesight. A few years back he just up and quit for awhile; said he found religion. He just started up again a couple months ago when the doc said he didn't have much time left. He turned ninety-five last month; still a scrapper though. He plays that damn old song just to torture himself."

When I asked Rat about the oars and life rings he said they were all Jack's idea. "The men whose names are painted on them were all friends of Jack's who went down with their ships. All were lost in Lake Superior over the years, just like Junior. Jack says when he dies, I have to put his body in my boat and take him out a couple miles and throw him overboard. He made me promise. He said if I wouldn't promise, he'd row out there on his own and jump in. Crazy old coot would too. Then he said he'd come back here and haunt my bar. He said he'd figure out how to talk to the animals and tell them when the cars were coming so they wouldn't get hit, and then I wouldn't have any meat for my chili. Crazy old fart. I'm going to miss him when he's gone."

"Are you going to take him out there when he dies?' I asked.

"Probably will, if I don't get caught," he said. "He made me promise."

Just then, Jack and Rat's wife walked in. "It sure is dark in here Rat. Didn't you pay the light bill? I can't hardly see a thing. Is that hippy still here?"

"I'm still here," I said, "I ain't going anywhere 'till I get that drink you promised me."

Rat left us to talk and went back to work in the kitchen. Jack asked him if he had been feeding me a load of crap while he was gone. And while he was speaking of crap, asked if there was any chili back there. It was suppertime and it sounded good. "Try some chili," Jack said, "It ain't half bad. Rat will try to tell ya it's beef, but I don't believe it. I saw him picking up road-kill last week. He had a porcupine and a deer in the back of his truck."

"You can't see past the end of your nose you old coot," Rat yelled from the kitchen. "Don't be starting rumors about my chili now. You'll scare away my dinner crowd. Two bowls coming right up."

As he sat the bowls on the counter, he told me not to let Jack talk my ears off. He said he had a whole bucket of ears he picked up off the floor and when Old Jack gets to talking, he don't shut up. Peoples' ears just fall off; it's one of them unexplained UP phenomena's. Jack just picked up his spoon and winked at me, "Careful you don't choke on no porky quill, and better stick some crackers in it to soak up the coon fat."

We ate our chili, and in fact, had a second bowl. Jack was right on both accounts, it was good chili and it wasn't beef. A couple folks came and went, and for several hours Jack told me a story— the story of Jack. He had me laughing so hard my side hurt. He talked about the things he did when he was younger, but when he got to the part about Junior, he got all serious. The smile left his face and a hollow look took its place. "It's my fault he died," he said. "My fault. I talked him into jumping on that dang ship. I should have let him buy that fishing boat. He might still be fishing today if it hadn't been for me. Man's got a right to fish."

"You can't blame yourself for that Jack. He was a grown man. He made that choice too."

"A man's got a right to feel guilty," he said, "it's called responsibility. I'm responsible and that's all there is to it. She don't give 'em back ya know. She's a greedy old hag."

"Who?" I asked. "Give what back?"

"Her dead. Old Lady Superior. She don't give up her dead. She holds them in her bosom like some old milk cow holds her last quart. She's got a heap of my friends too. And she'll have me here shortly if Rat stays true to his promise. Bring a couple of shots, Rat," Jack yelled. "It's about that time. Make it the good stuff, not that stuff I don't like. I may not be able to see what your pouring, but I can still taste ya know. Besides, we need something sweet to wash the porky out of our mouths after all that chili earlier."

Rat brought us our drinks and Jack got back to his story. "I came off the water when Junior died. I just up and retired. Searched for some answers in a bottle for awhile; wasted a few years drunk on my rear. Got so drunk one week, I messed my eyes all up. I don't see nothing now but shadows. Rat's wife, Mary, carts me around. Then one day Rat took me up to the Shipwreck Museum at Whitefish Point. I couldn't go in though. All those friends, and Junior; I just couldn't go in. But, this old preacher walked up to me in the parking lot and said I looked like I was hurting. Said he'd pray for me. 'Won't do ya no good' I told him. 'God's mad at me. I was supposed to protect that boy and I put him right on a death ship.' The preacher said he was sure God forgave me already and then he gave me this coin. I think it's got God's word on it."

He handed me a big copper coin marked with words. Not God's word, but I could see why he thought it. It read: *To reach the port of heaven, we must sail, sometimes with the wind, sometimes against it, but we must sail, not drift or lie at anchor.* "Oliver Wendell Holmes," Jack said. "He just gave me that coin and said if I'm looking for answers, I should try looking up. I didn't have another drink after that. Well, not 'till a couple months ago. Doc says I ain't got much time left, so what the heck, might as well treat myself. That old coin's got some wisdom on it. All them years of drifting, I never did steer toward heaven. Been having Rat's wife read a little Bible to me now and then, and it's all starting to make sense. If you want to get there, you must sail towards it. You gotta go looking; ya can't just drift around or drop anchor. Old Satin will blow you off course. He'll throw some storms at ya and then some waves. He'll even throw a crag up off the lake's floor just to snag ya up and try to get you to change course. But you gotta keep sailing. Every once in awhile you get a good wind, but it ain't easy. God is like a safe harbor and a harbor don't come looking for you. It's always there, but ya got to go find it. You can't drift into a harbor. The current always pushes you away from it. Satin is that current. He'll push you along real easy and if you ain't careful, he'll pull you under. Or maybe he'll throw up a fog bank so you get lost. That old preacher said all you need to stay on course is a Bible and a compass. I figure that Christ child is a lighthouse. Every once in awhile he throws out a beacon, but ya still gotta sail towards it. Yup, ya still gotta sail."

There it was, I thought. The lesson, although I wouldn't totally grasp it for a few years, a lesson just the same.

Rat was back in the kitchen cleaning up so Jack got up, went behind the bar and got himself a drink. He offered me one and as he sat the bottle down, he saw the sign about saving a fish.

He yelled back at Rat, "Is this that sign I asked you to get rid of Rat? I hate this sign."

He turned toward me and asked me to read it. I read to him what it said and he told me it wasn't very nice. "Man's got a right to fish," he said, "he's got a right to feed his family. The red man was here before we were. He's got a right to fish. Don't know about all those casinos, but he's got a right to fish. Says so right in the Bible—make fishers of men."

Rat came out of the kitchen and said he was ready to close up. It was past Jack's bedtime. Jack offered to meet me for breakfast and I readily accepted.

The next morning Jack was pretty quiet. He said he stayed up too late and wasn't feeling too perky. We talked for a short while and then it was time to hit the road. I thanked Jack for the talks and for the lesson, and told him to take care. He asked if I was heading right out and I told him as soon as I got a haircut. I was feeling a little hairy. He laughed , slapped me on the back and said, "Take care boys. Mind your Ps and Qs and whatever you do, sail. No matter the weather, just sail."

We pulled out of there and I never saw Old Jack again. That was many years ago and I'm sure he's long gone by now. If Rat kept his promise, Old Jack is lying two miles out at the bottom of the Superior. She'll keep him too, because she don't give up her dead. She holds them in her bosom like an old milk cow holds her last quart.

Steelies and the City Slicker (Crappy)

The alarm went off at 4 a.m. and no one stirred through the first two snooze alerts. Card playing and a few beers the night before had everyone slow to rise from their warm bunks. Then Steve was up making bodily noises that came from somewhere lower than his mouth. "Here's a kiss for all you wussies who can't hang with the big dogs," he said. He moved across the room leaving a foul stench that not only marked his territory but polluted the air.

"Oh man, you're sick," someone uttered from beneath his covers. "Go outside and do that." And with that, several stirred and a couple sunk deeper in their covers to avoid the awful smells that were escaping from Steve's body.

In an attempt to cleanse the air, I opened the door and put on the coffee, hoping the smell would fill the air with a more pleasant aroma, or at least reduce it enough so that we could go about getting ready without having to hold washcloths over our faces. After a few minutes, everyone was up and getting ready for what promised to be a good day on the river. As the slower few got ready, the rest of us rigged our rods and tied up a few spawn bags, filled our thermoses, and donned our waders. We loaded up and were off to the Big Manistee. We would be fishing just below Tippy Dam, as close as we could get to some of the holes we knew would hold those silver bullets. This morning we were fishing the south side of the river so we would have to walk down what seemed like a thousand steps to get to the water. I'm sure there weren't actually a thousand steps, but it always seemed that way when you were climbing back up at the end of a long day.

The parking lot was half full when we arrived so there were a few comments about how the beauty sleep didn't do any good anyway and tomorrow everybody better get around earlier. Of course, the words were directed at a select few, a select slower few. We reached the water and fired up our lanterns, and even though the temperature was in the teens, we were warmed by anticipation of scrapping, acrobatic, hard pulling trout at the other end of our lines. The action was slow until the eastern sky began to brighten and then the first "Fish on" was heard down river. We had a first time steelheader with us on this morning. I was kept busy with getting him ready and keeping him rigged-up because he had a unique ability to cast at, and get hung up on, every hungry rock and log on the bottom of the river, and every biting bush or tree on the bank behind him. Finally, I got my line into the water and as luck would have it, was soon into a battle with a frisky steelie. I led it to the net and then took it to scoop up another that my brother had fought close to shore. In the next hour or so several of us had caught (or lost) several fish and were having an awesome morning on the river. All except the first time steelheader, the city slicker who for the sake of anonymity we will call Crappy.

He hadn't had anything on his line other than rock or wood. I think I had rigged him up at least two dozen times and he still claimed he didn't know how to do it. I believe he just didn't want to take his hands out of his warm gloves. I told him this was the last time I was going to show him, so he'd better pay attention. I started to tie him up when I noticed he had turned around and started talking. I was fed up to my ears at this point so I tied the spawn bag directly to his line and did not put a hook on. "There you go. Good luck," I said. And with that, he cast out into the river.

As his line reached the end of his run, a steelie exploded at it and Crappy jerked his rod so hard it would have flung the fish clear up onto the bank had there been a hook on his line. "Darn," he said, "What did I do wrong?"

"For starters," I said, "You jerked too hard. And you'll catch more fish if you put a hook on the end of your line."

With that, he reeled in and sure enough, there was a busted spawn bag tied directly to his line. He shouted a few colorful words at me and then agreed he would give me his undivided attention as we re-rigged his rod. In the course of the next two hours, he tried everything in my vest, and in my box, but while everyone around him was hitting fish, he was still having absolutely no luck.

The coffee finally got the best of me so I went off into the woods to relieve myself. As I was taking care of business, I noticed a pile of deer berries there on the ground. I searched through my vest and found a small bag of rubber egg clusters that were labeled *Steelie Nuggets* and dumped them into a pocket. I then scooped up the deer berries, filled the bag, and put it back into my vest. I returned to the water and started fishing again only to notice Crappy was sitting on the bank. I asked him why he didn't have a line in the water and he stated that he had tried everything and nothing is working for him. "There are a lot of fish out there, and you're probably getting bites but don't realize it," I explained. I described how you just had to watch your line and give a little pull when you see it stop drifting down stream, especially if you see it start moving back up stream.

With that, he got up and started fishing again. After a few minutes I asked him what he was using and he said a wobble glow. I mentioned that I had something else to try but to come closer as I didn't want anyone else to hear. He wondered why we had to be so quiet so I explained that I had a secret bait that not too many people knew about. I further whispered that if everyone else was using this bait, then the fish would get wise to it and shy away. He agreed that it made perfect sense and would keep it to himself. "Promise," I said, "Swear you won't tell anyone?"

"I promise, and I swear I won't tell a soul," he said. "Now what do you have?"

I took the bag from my vest and handed it to him. "Steelie nuggets? Do they work?" he said.

"Give them a try and you tell me; but remember, it's a secret bait," I told him. He put one on each barb of his treble hook and then cast out.

When you fish the way we do at Tippy, you cast up stream and let your line drift down past you. As it nears the shore downstream, you retrieve it and start over again upstream. As you retrieve your line, you are reeling up right past the feet of ever fisherman downstream of you. Because of the amount of anglers on the river that morning, we were fishing fairly close together. We had, however, managed to keep all of us in a line so that we could fish together with a certain amount of timing and very few tangles with each other. As lines are retrieved past our feet, we tend to look as it passes in an attempt to see what other anglers are using, especially those who are catching fish. So, after Crappy finished his drift, he retrieved his line right past the feet of my three brothers as well as Steve, Larry, Neil, and the rest of the guys fishing with us. I could see the puzzled looks of each one of them as the line passed. Each time it drifted by, I could see it was drawing more interest, and finally someone asked, "Crappy, what are you using for bait?"

"You just never mind," he said, and then reeled faster to then cast out again. Every other time he brought in his line, he would have to put on new deer berries because the old ones had dissolved and washed off. With each retrieval of his line, I could see the interest was still growing, and was causing quite a discussion downstream. Finally, when my brother couldn't take it any more, he asked, "Dan, do you have Crappy fishing with deer poop?"

"Yeah," I said, "He'll try anything to get a fish."

"Deer poop?!" Crappy yelled, "I'm fishing with deer poop? I have to wash my hands. Where can I wash my hands?"

"You are standing in a river," I said.

"I need soap. Where can I get soap?" And with that, he walked up on the bank. "I can't stand it," he said, "I have to go to the gas station."

As he was leaving and starting for the steps to climb all the way back up, we all shouted out things we wanted him to pick up on his way back. He surely took his time getting back and for the rest of the week questioned everything we had him try. He did finally hook up with a couple fish, but got too excited and tried to horse them in (which is something you can't do when fishing with such light line). And believe it or not, the next time we went up fishing, he did go with us, and he did catch a fish. But that's another story.

The Slicker's First Steelie

The alarm went off at 4 a.m. and this time almost everyone was up and moving about. We had hit the river the night before and found it to be full of fish, and a warm rain promised to bring even more of those feisty silver bullets upstream. We filled our thermoses and tied up a few fresh spawn bags while the slowest still got their stuff together.

Everyone put on their waders and vests and we were in the trucks and on our way in record time (record time for this bunch of slowpokes). This morning we would be fishing the north side of the Tippy Dam. We had a long walk to where we were going so we decided we would leave the lanterns at camp. It was the first week of April and we knew it would already be crowded at the dam. Instead, we chose another spot downstream where we could spread out a bit and stay away from the confusion. We were on a mission to get the city slicker his first steelie, and we needed all the room we could get. He had a habit of hooking everything in sight, and everything out of sight, and we feared for the safety of nearby anglers once he commenced to casting. We were on the river and in the water by 5 a.m. and it was a beautiful morning. The steam was rising up off the water and the temp was around forty degrees. Because the weatherman promised us a clear day, we knew it would be overcast. A cloudy day would be perfect for these sun-shy steelies.

I helped the city slicker get rigged up and he was the first to get a cast off. He hooked up right off the bat and had a nice fight with an elm tree on the opposite bank. The tree won the battle and stole his rig. (For the sake of anonymity, we will again refer to the slicker as Crappy.) Well, Crappy reeled in, and with the help of yours truly, he got re-rigged. Then, in an ugly attempt to cast out, managed to stage war on the bushes above him. As before, he lost the fight and his rig, and was once again tying up. At this point, Crappy did some figuring in his head and said that at this rate his first fish was going to cost him over a thousand dollars. He didn't know if he could afford the three-limit catch.

"Fish on" was heard down stream and then shortly another came from upstream. Everyone decided to get their lines in the water as it has been proven that more fish are caught by those actually fishing, than those sitting on the bank. Besides, everyone figured it was safe for a few moments because Crappy was setting down and re-rigging. My brother Dave was into a fish on the first drift and let out a hearty "Fish on." Everyone got out of the water and he had all the room we thought he needed. The fish, however, had no intention of coming in and did a couple of tail-walks before deciding to head back towards Lake Michigan. It was stripping out line with no sign of slowing when Dave decided to end it. He broke his line and said, "Did you see how big he was? I couldn't even turn him. I think I had him hooked in the tail."

Well, Crappy was ready again. He came down between us and for Crappy, made an awesome cast. He actually hit the water and several of us congratulated him on his accomplishment. He shared a few choice words with us and continued his drift. His line started ripping back up stream without him noticing and my brother finally yelled, "Set the hook, Crappy. You have a fish on."

Crappy jerked his rod hard enough to turn the fish inside out. It came to the top of the water, splashed about, and then headed up stream. Crappy yelled for help, "What do I do now?" With the help of everyone shouting directions, he eventually got it under control. In a few short minutes, he led a nice six-pound male into the net. Crappy had the first fish of the morning and he was going to make sure everyone on the river knew it. You would have thought he caught a world record the way he bragged. He offered to give all of us lessons for a small fee and said for five dollars each, we could get our pictures holding it. For ten dollars, we could get our picture taken with him.

He rattled on and on about how he caught the monster and how we wished we could all be as good as he was at catching steelhead. Having had about enough of his noise, I told him the first one to catch a fish always went and got coffee to warm everyone up. He agreed and commented on how probably everyone in town, including the newspaper, would want to hear about his fish. "You're probably right," I said. "Make sure you tell everyone in town before you come back, and you might want to let those anglers in the next county know too."

With Crappy out of the way, it was now safe for the rest of us to get back into the water. Several comments were directed at me for bringing him up again this year, some of which were quite colorful and suggested what might happen if he found his way up next year. With all of us back in the water, we were soon into some fish. A couple nice ones were lost after a short battle, but then my brother hooked into a nice twelve-pounder that eventually came into the net. Soon after, I hooked into a strong male, also around twelve pounds, and managed to get him in and on the stringer. We usually let the females go, and only keep a male or two to smoke. A couple females were caught and released before we heard Crappy coming back down the bank. "How are all you Rookies doing? Are you ready for your lessons yet? Does anybody want me to show them where to cast?" This went on for a couple more minutes and then I couldn't take it any more.

"Hey Crappy, come over here close so I can enlighten you, or smack you upside the head."

"Oh Dan, you're just jealous. Do you want me to help you catch a fish?"

"Just shut up for a minute and listen. The guys here really like fishing with you, but you need to be a little more quiet. If they wanted to hear a lot of yelling, they would have stayed home and let their wives tell them how bad they fish. Besides, that fish you caught isn't even legal; it's too small."

"Yeah, you just say that because you can't catch one."

"Oh, I caught one, and mine is just barely legal. It's over there on the stringer with yours. Go take a look."

Crappy went over for a look and after a few minutes came back. "Wow, yours is bigger. Is mine really too small?"

"Yeah," I said. "They have to be a least ten pounds and yours is only six. The guys really like fishing with you and know how much this fish means to you, so they are willing to take a chance that we won't get caught." When Crappy asked what would happen if we were caught, I responded, "Well, we could lose our license and our gear, and maybe even our truck if they want to take it."

"Wow, those guys would do that for me? I can't let them get in trouble. I'm going to let it go."

"It's your call," I said, "Do what you have to." Crappy then went over to the stinger and took off his fish. He was holding it when I said, "Let me get a picture." But, just as I was getting my camera, my brother reminded Crappy that he better hang tight to that fish or it would get away.

"I like fishing with you guys and I don't want you to get in trouble over me, so I'm going to let it go. I know it's too small."

"What are you talking about being too small? It only has to be 16 inches. Dan, what are you telling him?"

"16 inches? Are you sure?" With that, Crappy put a hug on that fish that would have made any grandma proud. He ran twenty yards up the bank before he put it down. Then he turned around and started calling me everything but nice. He was jumping up and down like his pants were on fire and calling me everything that Webster refuses to print. We got a good laugh out of it and took some pictures; everyone congratulated him again on a nice fish. Someone then suggested he might want to mount that fish . . . and when he was done, he could take it to a taxidermist.

Good Old Days at Tippy Dam

If you have never been to northern Michigan to fish Tippy Dam, then you are missing out on a great adventure, for there is always something going on. My favorite time to be at Tippy is the tail end of winter or in early spring when the steelhead action is hot. Unfortunately, it is also everybody else's favorite time so it makes for some interesting days on the water. Tippy is also a favorite place of salmon fishermen in the fall and we often find the trash that is left behind after the snow melts and the waters go down. The bottom is always covered with heavy test line that was broken off in a fight with either a husky king or an unyielding river bottom full of snags. When I'm not in the river fishing, I quite often gather up this line and pile it on shore. Sometime I get enough to fill a large garbage bag that I carry out when we leave. Other times, I will pile a bunch of wood on top and start a campfire to warm our hands when the weather is dipping below freezing. The guys used to kid me about picking up the line, or ask me why I did it when it was not my mess in the first place. I would always reminded them that someone has to and I didn't see anyone else jumping up to do it. Besides, the river always rewards me. They would laugh and keep on fishing. On many occasions, I would leave the river with a bag of line in one hand and a nice steely in the other. It wasn't long before several of them started picking up the banks in hopes that the river would reward them; quite often, it would and several of them still do it to this day. My grandparents taught me to always leave the world a little nicer than I found it, so it has become a habit of mine, both on the river and in the woods.

On one particular morning, we were fishing up on the rocks near the boat launch on the north side of the river. There were a lot of fish holding out in front of us and we were having a great time. I hooked into a nice male and it tail-walked across the surface and then exploded down stream. I figured I had better go with it. I was walking across the large boulders with my rod tip high in the air trying to keep up with my fish. It was certainly trying his best to get back out to Lake Michigan. As I stepped on to a boulder, it rocked a little and I heard a loud squeal. I looked down and saw a brown tail flipping around. It then stopped and laid still. I followed the fish down to the boat launch where I was able to get it in after a short battle, and then put him on the stringer. As I was walking back to my fishing spot, I stopped at the boulder and there, beneath it, was a large male mink I must have killed when the boulder rocked forward. I picked him up and took him back to where we were fishing. The weather was fairly warm that day, so not wanting him to spoil, I put him on the stringer with our steelies and put them back in the icy water.

Awhile later a young boy was coming down the bank picking up old line and pulling it out of the water and off the rocks. I asked him what he was doing and he said that he was cleaning up the river as well as looking for some tackle that he could use to catch a steelie because he had never caught one before. Larry, who was fishing next to me, and I each thanked the young boy for doing such a great job of cleaning up the river. For his efforts, we both reached in our pockets and gave him five dollars to go buy tackle. He was very thankful, but said we didn't have to do that because he liked cleaning up the line.

He had his fishing pole with him so I invited him to fish with us awhile. I told him to look through my tackle boxes and whatever he liked, we could tie on his line and get him set up. He picked out a clown-colored wobble glow and we soon had him rigged up. I told him to get right up where I was standing and gave him my polarized glasses so he could see the fish. We guided him on how to fish and where to cast, and he was soon into a large male that was hell bent on going down stream. We went with him. I grabbed a net and after a long battle, we had his first steelhead in the net. I handed him the fish and he dropped his rod and took off running upstream with his fish. Somewhat stunned, I picked up his rod and took it back to where we were fishing.

A few minutes later, he came back with his dad. "These are the guys right here, Dad. They'll tell you that I caught this fish. Just ask them."

We confirmed he was telling the truth and that he did it all by himself. "You have got to be kidding," his dad replied. "I have been up here for six years now trying to catch one and I still can't get one in the net."

I suggested he take some lessons from his son because he was quite a fisherman. He just laughed and said he would. The boy asked if he could hang around and watch us fish for awhile; of course, we said okay. He went down and looked at our stringer and saw that mink there in the water and asked what it was. "Why, that's an Alaskan fur bearing trout, Son. They are pretty rare," I said.

He smiled and said it looked more like a drowned cat. He had a lot of fun with it. Every time someone would walk by, he would ask if they knew what an AFBT was. Most of them said they never heard of such a thing. "Why that's an Alaskan fur bearing trout," he'd say. "You sure you never heard of one? Let me show you what one looks like." We all got quite a kick out of it, and had a nice morning on the river.

Another morning at Tippy, we woke to fresh snow and temperatures dipping down into the teens. We decided to get a warm breakfast in us first and five o'clock found ourselves in the restaurant gulping down coffee and hot food. I noticed an elderly women sitting by herself in the corner, eating toast and drinking some tea. She looked pretty worn and tired so I asked the waitress if she was okay. She informed me that the woman was okay, but had just lost her husband a couple weeks ago. She comes in for breakfast every morning. "That doesn't look like much breakfast to me. Is that all she eats?"

"That's all she can afford because her husband was disabled and hadn't worked in several years. He spent all his time walking the river and picking up trash, and sometimes the park rangers would pay him."

All of the sudden there was a hollow feeling inside of me, like I had never felt before; I felt I had to do something. I reached in my wallet to find only forty dollars. I had to still get home so I asked my buddy if he could spot me some cash until we got back. I called the waitress over and handed her the forty dollars, asking her to give the woman what she wanted for breakfast every morning until the money was gone. "Why?' she asked, "You don't even know her."

"She's my kind of people," I said, "and she reminds me of my grandmother. Just tell her it's from the rangers. I can trust you to do this, can't I?'"

She said she thought I was weird, but yes, I could trust her. We finished our breakfast and went down to the river. It was bitter cold with the wind blowing down the riverbed and icing up our rod tips after every other cast, but I was warm that morning and as comfortable as I have ever been on the river. My fingers were warm and I even managed to catch a steelhead, the only one on the river that morning. So, like I always say, "The river takes care of those who take care of it."

One morning we were on the north side fishing on the rocks just above the launch when a little girl who couldn't have been more than four was making her way down the river. She was playing close to the water's edge, jumping from boulder to boulder. There was still a little snow on the ground and some of the rocks were icy; the water was just above freezing and rather high. As she got closer, I told her she needed to be careful and get away from the water so she wouldn't fall in. She said her daddy said it was okay and she wasn't scared. I asked her where her daddy was and she told me he was up by the dam where the little waterfall is. The only waterfall around was the little cofferdam and that was over a hundred yards away. A man standing behind us noted that he saw them when they arrived, and he knew what her father looked like and he offered to go find him. Soon after, the girl was still jumping across the boulders when she slipped and fell into the water. The current had a hold of her and was quickly taking her down stream about ten feet off shore. Several fishermen were trying to grab her as she went by. We ran down to the launch and I waded out as far as I could before the bottom dropped off. My buddy Jimmy held on to my hand and as she got close, I was able to lunge forward and grab hold of her and Jimmy pulled us back into shallower water. We took her up to the parking lot, wrapped her in a sleeping bag, and started up the car to get her warm.

News of the little girl swept up the bank like wildfire, and yet it still took twenty minutes before her dad arrived at the car. I saw him walking toward the car and to myself, thought he should be in more of a hurry. When he got to the car, he yelled at her and told her she should have been more careful. One of the men standing there said, "No, you should have been more careful."

I asked if she had warm clothes and her father said she'd be alright and that maybe she learned something from falling in the water. I told him she wouldn't be all right and could easily get hypothermia. He said it would serve her right and that I shouldn't tell him how to take care of his own child. Every muscle in my body wanted at that very minute to hit him upside the head and knock some sense into him, but that little girl was scared and I didn't want to add to her fears. A couple of the other fishermen were arguing with him when the police arrived. They placed him in their car and got the little girl dried off and warmed up until the mother came and took her home. The dad stayed there and tried to keep fishing, but every fisherman on the river was making it most unpleasant for him. When he finally did give up and leave, we all applauded as he left.

Another time we were up there several weeks earlier than usual because of un-seasonal weather. The steelhead were in and so were the walleye. The walleye that come in to Tippy to spawn are huge, often over ten pounds. We quite often catch them when fishing for steelhead and have to let them go because the season is usually closed. My best friend is an avid walleye fisherman and on this particular morning happened to tie into a very large one. He fought it for a short time and then managed to get it into a net. He picked it up and said, "This is a monster. It's the biggest one I've ever caught. I wish I could keep it, but I had better let it go."

I asked if he wanted his picture taken and he declined saying he would wait for a legal one and just get it mounted. My brother stated that it sure was a beauty and would look nice on the wall. "Yeah, it sure would, but I better get it back in," Steve said as he laid it in the water and watched it swim away.

"I think I would have kept that one. It was a beauty," my brother mentioned again.

"I think I would have too. You don't see too many hogs like that," I added.

Steve replied, "Yeah, I would have liked to, but you know the season is closed." My brother and I just laughed and informed him that the season wasn't closed for another two weeks. We came up a month early. At that point, I think I saw fire come from his mouth and ears as he yelled at us for not stopping him from letting it go. We just told him that we hadn't caught one that big yet, and didn't want to hear his fish story every time we came over to his house and saw it on the wall. If he would have been driving, I believe he would have left us on the river. He took it in good stride though and the rest of the weekend he fished for walleye instead of steelhead. Never did he catch one. Oops, I guess we should have told him sooner.

The following story uses the word "nigger" in it. It is a word I don't like. It is one of those offensive words that are often used to inflict pain. I apologize if it offends anyone because that is not my intention. I asked my friend that was there that day if I should use it and he said it should be included. He said it was because of the word that the morning played out like it did.

.

[177]

Another year, my buddy Steve and I decided to bring a friend up
with us. We had fished with him for several years for pan-fish
and salmon, but he had never been steelheading. He was a little
apprehensive about going because it was so far up north and he
was a black man and he might be out of place. We assured him
that it would be okay and he would be among friends. He agreed
and we headed up. We got there early in the week and fished a
couple days before Friday rolled around. On Friday, it got really
crowded and it was hard to find a spot. So, we told ourselves
we would be there early on Saturday.

The next morning, we arrived well before first light and were
fishing long before the other anglers started to filter in. A couple
of older gentlemen were across the river from us and they had
tied into a couple, only to lose them. Shortly after it got light,
four younger fishermen came down and squeezed in between
the two older men, eventually pushing them out of their spot.
The older men got up and moved a little ways down river where
there was more room. One of the guys across the river tied into
a steely and fought it for a couple minutes, but then lost it. I
laughed to myself and thought he deserved to lose it after forc-
ing those men out. He started getting loud and yelling and was
really getting annoying when one of his buddies told him to
quiet down a little because he might be bothering some of the
other fishermen who were enjoying the peace and quiet. Some-
one else down river yelled back that it would be nice if he were
a little bit quieter. The loud one yelled back some obscenities
and told him if he was man enough, he could come down there
and shut him up. Now, he was starting to get on my nerves. He
was being loud, had pushed two older men out of their fishing
hole, and was looking for a fight. Not wanting a confrontation
so early in the morning, I held my tongue. But then he opened
his mouth again and that was the last straw.

He yelled at the top of his lungs that he had a right to be loud
because he was up north in white man's territory and there
weren't no niggers. I looked over at my buddy and saw him
cringe. That was enough. I yelled back that it was God's terri-

tory and we were all enjoying the peace and quiet until an idiot showed up. He yelled back that I must be a nigger-lover and that maybe I should pack up and go back home to Detroit or wherever I came from. My buddy told me to let it go, that it didn't matter; but to me, it did. I brought him up here and I felt responsible to show him a good time. I yelled across the river that maybe he should go back to his plantation and leave us to the quiet weekend we came up to enjoy. He was screaming up a storm, making several others upset. All were all asking him to just shut up or leave. Then he yelled back that if there were some nigger lovers out there who were man enough to shut him and his buddy up, they should come across the river and try. I yelled back that I would be right over and turned around to wade back to shore and put my rod down. My buddy Steve told me he had my back and then my younger brother said, "I'm right there with you two."

"Let it go," my black friend said. But I just couldn't. I took off my vest and gloves and turned around to go across the river. And then, I couldn't believe my eyes. Eight guys were already ahead of me wading across the river.

The guy with the big mouth and one of his buddies picked up their stuff and left the river before any of us got to their side. The other two apologized for their friend being such an idiot and asked if we minded them staying. One of the guys wading across the river said there were a couple of older guys there before so maybe they should ask them. One of them then went down river and came back with the two older men, giving them back their hole back.

The rest of the day was a lot of fun with everybody tying into fish and having a good time. Six of the guys wading across the river were either family, long time fishing and hunting buddies, or guys we saw up there every year who we enjoyed fishing with. The other two were complete strangers. I asked one why they were willing to stick up for a stranger, and willing to fight. He told me that on Thursday when they were looking for a place to fish because the river was so crowded, my black friend invited them to slip in next to him and moved over to make room. He said they talked all morning and that he seemed like a really good person. That's why they were back here fishing next to us this morning.

"He is a good person, and you're a very good judge of character," I said.

We fished along side each other for awhile and as I stood there among all these guys, I really felt proud. The reason I so much liked to be up there with these men was because they were just that—real men. They judged a man by his character and his integrity, not by his background or skin color. I knew that morning that if I crossed that river, I wouldn't be alone. I knew my brother had my back and my buddy would be right there with us. But I never dreamed those other guys would beat me across. After I stop to think about it, I guess I'm really not surprised.

"I have a dream that my children will not be judged by the color of their skin, but by the weight of their character."

~ Martin Luther King

"I don't like that man. I must get to know him better."

~ Abraham Lincoln

"Sticks and stones can break your bones but words will never hurt you." Wrong. Sticks and stones may break your bones or bruise you, but those, in time can mend. Yet, words do hurt and they can bruise your spirit and most definitely leave their mark, and all too often never heal.

~ Author

Behind a Father's Eyes

The wedding day is finally here
Your wife and daughter say "At last"
But you're mumbling underneath your breath
"This day got here too darn fast"

As you're setting up for the reception
And mumbling about the cost
You're wishing you were fishing
Another vacation day is lost

Your future son-in-law walks by
Dressed up in his rented tux
Do you think he knows in her daddy's eyes
He will never measure up

Every fiber in your body
Wants to yank him from that room
And have a little man-to-man
Just the father and the groom

To offer up an explanation
Of what his new life has in store
Like if he ever laid a hand on her
You'll be breaking down his door

Yet you know how much she loves him
And you guess he'll never know
Until he has a daughter
That it's so hard to let them go

You try hard to give a stern look
To put some fear in that boy's eyes
But it's hard to look too fearful
With those darn tears in your eyes

Then you see your own reflection
A look you've seen a time or two
It was the look back on your wedding day
Your wife's daddy gave to you

And then they call you in the chapel
And she's standing there in white
Stained glass windows up above you
Are bathing her in heaven's light

Then your heart stops for a moment
It's only done that once before
It was the day you wed her mother
As she came walking through that door

And now everything is clearer
Because you've come to realize
There's more love than meanness lurking
Behind a father's eyes

And soon the preacher man's up front
With the party and the groom
And as the music starts to play
Every head turns in that room

You have your daughter on your arm
And you turn to face the crowd
You realize in that moment
That you've never been so proud

You walk her down the chapel aisle
And as you hand her to her man
You notice how he looks at her
And you finely understand

There is a smile upon your daughter's face
Like you've never seen before
Every penny now was worth it
Even if it had cost more

The wedding goes without a hitch
And soon you're out there on the floor
Dancing with your daughter
Something you've never done before

She kisses you upon your cheek
And she thanks you for the day
Emotions make it hard to speak
And you simple say "Okay"

And soon the celebration's over
The bride and groom are gone
Everything's packed in your car
You and your wife are headed home

The ride is fairly quiet
Perhaps because the day was long
Or is it the realization
That your child is finally gone

You find yourself alone that night
Just sitting on her bed
As memories turn like pages
In the book you call your head

And you wonder in the years that passed
Did you give her all she needs
And as you think about her future
You get down on your knees

[183]

Then you ask the Lord to guide them
Through a world that can be tough
And pray they stick together
When the road starts to get rough

You ask for years of happiness
Prosperity and love
And that He bless this couple
And guide them from above

You realize she's a woman now
You may not see her for awhile
But you draw strength remembering
The love in your girl's smile

And as you think about their wedding night
You realize a brand new fear
You're too young to be a grandpa
You hope they wait a couple years

Count Your Blessings

On the way to work last Monday
Thinking what a wasted day
I would rather be out fishing
Where I could cast my cares away

I saw a young man at the corner
His sign read "Will work for food"
And here I am complaining
When my life is so dang good

I've got a job, a wife who loves me
Two daughters and two sons
And I woke up again this morning
Awe man, I'm the lucky one

My daddy died when just a young man
From cancers brought back from a war
I never heard that man complaining
Or ask what he was dying for

Awhile back I lost a best friend
Who left two daughters and a wife
A failing kidney stole my buddy
From the three loves of his life

Like my father he had courage
Through all the hurt and pain he felt
I never once heard him complaining
About the hand that he was dealt

Special Olympics were last weekend
A friend and I dropped in
There was an air of great excitement
'Cuz everybody there could win

[185]

The very struggles each was going through
Would have broke this lesser man
But each raised their arms in victory
Because they did the best they can

I went out behind the bleachers
And I got down on my knees
And thanked God for the blessings
He gave a hypocrite like me

Thank their creator for their blessings
Is what everyone should do
Because you don't have to look far
To find someone worse off than you

I was at the store the other day
In the aisle next to the toys
When I heard the laughs and giggles
Of a happy little boy

I stuck my head around the corner
To see what was going on
I saw him sitting in a wheelchair
And both his legs were gone

I went back to the bottle room
And I got down on my knee
And again thanked my Creator
For the gifts He gave to me

Awhile back I grabbed a paper
Bold and black the headlines read
Another roadside bomb exploded
It left four soldiers dead

They fought for freedom in a country
For folks they didn't even know
And here I was complaining
Because the weather looked like snow

I've got a house and property
A pickup in the drive
Unlike those boys who died for freedom
I'm still very much alive

So if you see me on the street
Whining about my woes and strife
Please remind me of the blessings
God has given me in life

And if I keep complaining
Feel free to slap me on my face
For I'm nothing but ungrateful
And I don't deserve His grace

"I don't think of all the misery but of all the
beauty that still remains."
~ Anne Frank

"O my friend, it is not what they take away from you
that counts. It is what you do with what you have left."
~ Hubert Humphrey

"Life brings sorrows and joys alike. It is what a man does with
them, not what they do to him, that is the true test of his mettle."
~ Theodore Roosevelt

Change My Destiny

Have you ever wondered what it was
That your existence lacked?
Did your mind ever wander
And have a hard time coming back?

That's how I felt this morning
Until there came a gentle breeze.
It filled the room around me
And seemed to beckon "Follow me."

It pulled at me down deep inside
Like cheese attracts a hungry mouse.
And so I followed it outside
To the woods behind our house.

It led me far, far from my home
Way out among the trees.
And there, something seemed to beg
"Look here among the leaves."

I saw an acorn lying there
Exposed upon the ground.
And thought what might become
Of this treasure that I found.

I pushed it down into the earth
And changed its destiny.
For what might have been a squirrel's meal
Could now become a tree.

Then something seemed to draw me
As if I was being led.
To a place inside that woods
Where red birds circled overhead.

A cardinal fledging flopped about
Upon the forest floor.
Fallen from its lofty nest
Up where its parents soared.

I picked it up with soft-gloved hand
So as not to leave my scent.
And climbed and placed it where it was
Before its accident.

I realized then that I was lost
Within this wooded glen.
But something seemed to pull at me
And lead me on again.

I came across a trickling creek
Its waters much too low.
The minnows gathered in still pools
Where water used to flow.

Afraid the sun might dry them up
I made a small rock dam.
The water rose and made a pond
Where soon those minnows swam.

As the water trickled over the rocks
It played a melody.
So I sat down on the bank to hear
And soon was fast asleep.

The waters noises stirred my mind
And dreams were coming fast.
Each represented choices
That I made within my past.

They came and went like fluffy clouds
On a warm and breezy day.
Then I awoke refreshed and felt
My burdens slip away.

I sat and pondered how this day
So paralleled my life.
And how the choices that I make
Affect my children and my wife.

Like the man who missed the forest
Because of all the trees.
The answers to all my questions
Were right there in front of me.

The woods was mediocrity
That I was lost within.
Resigned to fate, my dreams were gone
It seemed I'd given in.

That fledging was my lovely wife
I took for granted for so long.
She'd fallen from her pedestal
Where she very much belonged.

I needed to help her back again
Where she deserved to be.
And hold up the promises I made
The day she married me.

That trickling creek with waters low
Was just the circumstance.
That I created in my life
Afraid to take a chance.

Content within my comfort zone
Afraid to step outside.
I created those shallow pools
Where my family would reside.

Those minnows were my family
And yes, I swam there too.
Afraid to go and do those things
I knew that I should do.

And like that tiny acorn
I could just resign to fate.
And be just another lowly nut
Or maybe squirrel bait.

Instead of laying there content
Within mediocrity.
I need to get a little dirty
To be all that I can be.

I might get stepped on a time or two
Before I start to grow.
But then the sky's the limit
And I can reach my goals.

If it is to be, it's up to me
To change my destiny.
And have a life where I can live
Just my priorities.

I've a beauty I must rescue
A battle I must fight.
An adventure I must live
To make circumstances right.

If I'm a humble student
And do the best I can.
I know I have a purpose
Somewhere in God's plan.

It wasn't chance that brought me down
This wooded path today.
For I was lost within the woods
'Till God showed me the way.

"So often times it happens, we live our lives in chains
and we never even know we have the key."
~ The Eagles, *Already Gone*

"Most people today have the means to live by, but they don't
have a meaning to live for."
~ Victor Frankel

Fallen Heroes

The list of fallen heroes who gave their life for us and our country is endless. Such unselfish individuals who gave their all so we may have a quality life and a chance at a better future. So we might wake up each morning in a free country and enjoy life to the fullest; So we have freedoms that no other country has, like freedom of speech, the freedom of religion, and the right to bear arms. Our forefathers knew how important these rights were when they wrote the Constitution and the Bill of Rights, and they wanted them for each of us.

Of all the rights bestowed on us as citizens, I believe these three are the most important to me. The freedom of speech gives me the right to say what is on my mind and in my heart without the threat of prosecution. In so many other countries, that would be a problem. Bearing arms gives me the right to pick up a gun to protect my family and to go out into the woods to hunt. Freedom of religion, which gives me the right to worship as I choose, was why this nation was founded. This right gives me the honor to worship the one true God and also my greatest hero, My Lord and Savior Jesus Christ. He lived a perfect, sinless life and in spite of that, or because of that, he was hung on a cross to die. A crown of thorns was pushed onto his head to mock him. Nails were driven through his hands and feet and a sword thrust into his side. He hung there in agony to release me of my sins and allow me the right to enter into the kingdom of heaven just by believing in him. As he hung there dying he didn't condemn anyone for putting him there. He knew it was in God's plan to set us free and he gladly gave his life for us. Like so many of our soldiers, he gave his all for us and we so often take that for granted.

The Greatest Hero

Two thousand years ago there lived
A man who walked this earth
He said he was the son of God
Born of a virgin birth

He didn't sin, hurt anyone
He didn't steal or lie
Why then you ask, this gentle soul
Was he condemned to die

They braided up a crown of thorns
Placed it hard upon his head
From every thorn that pierced his face
There flowed a crimson red

His crimson blood flowed freely
Across his body down the tree
The very blood he gave the world
To save a wretch like me

I helped to place him on that tree
My sins, my deeds, my lies
He lived the life I couldn't live
He died the death I should have died

Yes my transgressions put him there
My sins helped drive those nails
For the imperfect life I lived
His precious side impaled

He is a hero in my book
He gave his life to save my soul
He didn't even know me
Two thousand years ago

As for me, I'm just a mortal
An ordinary man
A sinner in a sinful world
I do the best I can

He asks only that I believe
Have faith, He died for me
And when my time has come to pass
My soul He will set free

And it will soar up to the heavens
Up to that holy place
Where I will bask in all His glory
As I look upon His face

Two thousand years ago there lived
A man who walked this earth
He truly was the son of God
Born of a virgin birth

And on that hill far, far away
Hung on that dogwood tree
My dear Savior was crucified
He gave His life for me

Be True to Yourself

There is a moral fiber
Entwined in each of us
That little voice that says "That's wrong"
We know when it is just

We understand the do's and don'ts
They're morals planted in our soul
But often times we turn our head
And that creates a hole

We're taught to do the right thing
When passing through our youth
Live our life with character
Always speak the truth

So when we gaze into a mirror
We don't see a stranger's face
But someone we are proud of
Is reflected in that space

And know integrity and trust
Is packed within our shell
So that we're saved and heaven-bound
Not destined straight to hell

Today is all we truly have
Be it peace or joy or sorrow
Yesterday is behind us
We've no promise of tomorrow

So live life in the moment
That's what we need to do
Fulfill our purpose on this earth
Do what we're destined to

Our world is full of roadblocks
They try to change our ways
But if we stay true to ourselves
We'll have victories every day

The world can be an ugly place
Satan is a mighty foe
But if we go in kindness
We'll reap a smile wherever we may go

So keep that smile upon your face
Make that your weaponry
And arm yourselves with kindness
For all the world to see

We just may change this country
It's not too late to start
The first step is to search ourselves
Look into our own hearts

Would the child we used to be
Be proud of who we are today
And if we saw God face-to-face
What would He have to say

Would He say we filled the purpose
He'd intended for our lives
And have we done the best we could
For our children and our wives

All questions we must answer
When searching for the truth
And lessons learned we now must share
With those we call our youth

So walk the talk from day to day
Put your ego on the shelf
Be the best that you can be
And be true to yourself

"I have decided to stick with love. Hate is too great
a burden to bear."

~ Martin Luther King

Stop and Smell the Roses

As a kid, I remember more than once an old timer (as we called them) saying, "Just slow down and stop and smell the roses." I'd walk away thinking, "I could slow down if I wanted, but I don't want to smell no stinking flower, and I don't have to listen to you anyway." That was back when summer was too short and the school week was too long. It seemed like Christmas break was a long time in coming and spring break was a lifetime away. I don't have to plan for the future; shoot, I can't even see past Friday night. I don't have time to slow down until I get to twenty-one.

Then came the short jog to adulthood where all my worries were supposed to slip away. It seemed like it took forever, but I made it. Hooray, here I am. I'm legal now, and I can buy alcohol. Someone asks you what you're going to do with your life and the only answer you have is "party." The next few years are a blur and somehow you find your way on the train to middle aged. She's a speedy one but you manage to jump off at thirty and get a little cottage in the woods. You set back in your Lazy Boy and kick your feet up; and just when you start to get comfortable, you hear it. You look out the window and there it is, a great big truck with *Welcome to The Real World* painted on the side. It backs up to your front door and dumps a whole load of responsibility on your front stoop. You're left standing there in the dust and you can barely read the license plate that says *Sucker*. You find yourself running after it screaming, "Wait a minute! This isn't all mine; take some back. I had a dream." You shovel it all into bags, label it baggage, and drag it to the train station and board the highball to forty. You jump off at forty, use the bathroom, and when you're washing your hands, you see yourself in the mirror. You make a mental note to work out and get in shape and then you close your eyes for a second. You wake up to someone screaming, "Welcome to fifty. You're in the county of the middle-aged." Around your neck they throw a lei with flowers that are already wilted. And to top it off, you forgot to go to the gym.

The last two decades flew by like Old #3 on a hot track with Dale Earnhart at the wheel. You barely had time to catch your breath, let alone take the nap your body keeps hinting you need. I have a theory, and it's only a theory, but in my simple mind, it makes perfect sense. I believe that somewhere between thirty and forty we slip into a parallel universe. We are still here but in a different dimension where the earth is spinning faster. The days and weekends are shorter and you get tired quicker. Seasons fly by in a hurry and you're just getting the last of the summer clothes out of the box when it's time to put on the snow boots. All the mirrors in this universe are carnival mirrors, making you look shorter and stouter. Someone says middle aged isn't just a metaphor, it's a disease that causes everything to gravitate to your middle and gather there; hence the name of middle-aged.

"Stop and smell the roses" seems like good advice now, and you wish one of those old-timers would have grabbed you by the ear and said, "Don't sass me. Respect your elders, shut up, and pay attention. I'm serious." Then you have an epiphany: Wait a minute, I am one of those old-timers. All of a sudden you realize that your parents were right, and somewhere in a closet you find the courage to tell them so, because in this new world, pride takes a back seat to reality. They don't rub it in because they were there once. Heck, they blazed the trail that you somewhat followed. Besides they're on the same ride you're on and when you ask for advice all they can say is "Hold on. It gets pretty wild."

All of a sudden there you are at fifty and you're still looking for answers. Don't get me wrong; I'm glad I made it this far. I've lived with mortality all my life never expecting to live past thirty-six. I truly thought I would follow in my father's footsteps, but I've already outlived him by fifteen years. I feel guilty, but I'm thankful, and I know I'm blessed. Everyday is a gift to me and I appreciate it. At fifty you realize just how fragile life is because you've lost some loved ones, many of them younger than you are now. You begin to realize how precious time is. You would like to stop and smell the roses and you know you better do it quickly or life might just rear-end you in the britches if you stop too long.

Zero to fifty is a pretty good ride even though there's a lot of rough track along the route. If you're lucky, you'll meet someone along the way and she'll smile back at you. You'll buy her dinner and feed her some lies and con her into saying "I do." And then if you're really lucky, she'll stick it out and hang with you through all the storms that blow up and get in your way. She'll forgive you for your shortcomings when she realizes that you both lost track of your dreams. She won't mind that the tires on her car are wearing thin or that the one around your waist is over-inflated. If she does mind, she'll hide it well and God bless her for not rubbing it in. She knows her man is a straight ball hitter and that they keep throwing him curves. She knows there are other pitchers out there but she has faith that you'll get a hit off them if you don't run out of innings. She helps you to your feet when you fall and fluffs your pillow so you have a soft place to lay down your head. She's a Godsend, and chances are you've never told her. Maybe some kids find there way into your lives. If they do, chances are they're just as much a handful as you. You love them and yell at them and they don't want to listen any better than you did. One day they're crawling up on your knee and the next they're pushing you away saying "I'm an adult now. Don't tell me what to do." Sound familiar? Then they're walking down the aisle with a new love and your left hoping for grandkids to fill the void. That's life in the fast lane.

Fifty is good, really it is, and fifty-one is better. With any luck you'll have more victories than regrets. When I got there I realized that change is the only constant, and I changed a lot. Somewhere along the way my waistline gained more inches than my inseam. I gained some weight and I gained some wisdom. I learned some lessons—in the form of mistakes—along the way, but I'm smart enough now to know that if I walk away wiser, then they weren't really mistakes after all. I know now how precious time shared with loved ones is, and truth be told, that's my biggest regret. Visiting a grave doesn't give you the chance to say "I love you and I appreciate you. Thank you for being a part of my life." You can say it, and I'd like to believe they still hear it, but I don't get that same jolt of satisfaction that I do when I say it face-to-face. In fact, I feel like I cheated them by not telling them when I had the chance. Kiss your aunts and hug your uncles. Go see your parents and grandparents because they could be gone when you wake up tomorrow. Nike is on to something when they say *Just do it*. Don't think about it, just do it or you'll end up feeling guilty and lonely. You keep telling yourself you'll get around to seeing them and then all of a sudden they're gone. It ought to be a crime. If you're like me, the judge would find you guilty. Your only defense would be that life got in the way. When he slams the gavel down, you're sentence is a life of heartache that eats at you the rest of your days. You beat yourself up for not getting in the car and going to see them. Your only hope of parole is if insanity or Alzheimer's sets in and you forget how selfish you were with your time. Hindsight is twenty-twenty, but the boot that kicks you in the butt is a size sixteen, triple-d. It's pointed and relentless. It forces a hole in you where little by little your self-worth leaks out and leaves you feeling empty and jaded.

Life in this parallel universe becomes more precious when you discover that time is the only commodity that matters. Every decade that passes seems to speed up just when you want time to slow down. You want to scream it from the mountain tops - "Stop and smell the roses." You want to tell the world, or at least your kids, to shut up and listen. You feel like an old hound that's been out all night howling at the moon and nobody hears you. I know what I'm talking about. I was there. I lived it. I don't want you to make the same mistakes I did. So pay attention. If you don't want the pain that accompanies regret, then go see your loved ones. Tell your friends what they mean to you; it doesn't hurt and no one is keeping track of how sappy you get. Really, it's okay.

The Eagles said it best in *Already Gone*: *So often times it happens, we all live our lives in chains, and we never even know we have the key.* Victor Frankel said, "Most people today have a means to live by, but they don't have a meaning to live for." Make your loved ones that meaning. If we die today we will probably be replaced at work tomorrow, but never ever in our families' lives. So why is it that we spend so much time at work and so little with the ones that really matter? Go see someone you care about today and tell them just that. Call in sick if you have to; I won't tell anybody. And remember, every time you smile you unconsciously give someone else permission to do the same. There is a richness in family that can never be compared to money, a wealth in friendship that has everything to do with life and nothing to do with material things. "I appreciate your friendship. Thank you for being a part of my life." Thirteen little words when strung together that can change your life. It doesn't hurt to say them, but the smiles they bring would be worth it even if it did. Go on, get out of here. What are you waiting for? Go hug somebody, and on the way, stop and smell the roses.

In Parting

Heroes today are few and far between in our country. That needs to change.

This country was founded on certain principles and moral values that are now being stepped on and taken away right in front of our eyes. And we do nothing as a people. Over a million men and women have given their lives to protect what we are so eager to give away. The freedom of religion, the right to bear arms, the freedom of speech, and freedom itself are just a few. There is still hope for this nation if good men and women step up to the task. Stand up for what you think is right; stand up for the underdog; go about your day with integrity and live your life with character. Then we can put this nation back on track. It takes a person of character and integrity, a person of moral value and courage with a love of family and country, to be a leader. That is each and every one of us if we only look deep enough.

We live in the greatest country in the world and we so often take it for granted. We as a people need to stand up and make a little noise, and then they will listen because everyone loves a hero, everyone yearns for a hero, and anyone of us can be that to someone. Changing the world is like eating an elephant. You have to do it one bite at a time. One person here steps up, and one person there, and another over there, and soon we have heroes popping up everywhere and things will begin to change for the better. What have we got to lose by trying? Nothing, but we have everything to gain.

John Quincy Adams said, "You will never know how much your freedom has cost my generation. I hope you don't squander it." Let us be the generation that turns this country around and heads it in the direction our forefathers dreamed of and died for. Let it not be said that we squandered it.

In the Bible, The Book of Isaiah 1:17 says, "Seek justice, encourage the oppressed, defend the cause of the Fatherless, and plead the case of the widow." And in his awesome book "Season of Life," Jeffrey Marx quotes football legend Joe Ehremann as saying, "Wherever there is injustice we ought to show up, stand up, and speak up. Because whenever we can show up, stand up, and speak up, that's when we start changing the world."

You've heard it said before, "Evil can only flourish when good men stand by and do nothing." Let's take Joe's advice and show up, stand up, and speak up for the principles this country was founded on. It's our responsibility to leave this country better off than we found it. Go be a hero to someone and leave your legacy. Pay it forward like our forefathers did. We honor our past with a memory; we should honor our future with action.

There are many leaders and heroes in communities throughout this country who are trying to make a difference. They practice brotherhood, peace, love, and responsibility. They live a code of ethics and have character and integrity, but because they are not angry or violent enough, they are not newsworthy to our media. That's where we are failing as a country—when we look only for the bad in our lives and not for the positives. The men and women I've talked about within these pages are some of those people. They are on the side of what is right and just, and they are trying to make a difference. They don't go looking for a fight, but I know they are not afraid to bleed for what they believe. They will stand up for their rights, and for the underdog. And if a fight breaks out, they will stand strong. When the fight is over and they tally up the wounded, you will find no wounds in their backsides because they will never turn and run. They are not cowards; they are heroes and many of them are you. Courage is not the lack of fear; it is doing the right thing in spite of those fears.

When the time comes and they try to take away our rights, I hope we recall our ancestor's sacrifices, the lives of men and women soldiers who were lost defending these rights, and what our children and our children's children stand to lose.

The time has come for us to make that difference; they are trying to take away the rights we hold dear. The freedom takers are knocking at our door. But I know like true Americans, you will stand with me in defiance and say "Not on our watch you don't! No, not on our watch!"

God bless.

Made in the USA
Charleston, SC
14 February 2010